NITI Aayog and Planning Commission

Some Reflections

NITI Aayog and Planning Commission

Some Reflections

K.D. Saksena

SHIPRA

Rs. 995; US$ 40

ISBN: 978-93-88691-04-8

First Published in India in 2019

NITI Aayog and Planning Commission: Some Reflections

Published by:
SHIPRA PUBLICATIONS
LG 18-19, Pankaj Central Market
I.P. Ext., Patparganj, Delhi 110092, India
Tel.: +91 11 2223 5152/6152
E-mail: info@shiprapublication.com
www.shiprapublication.com

Dedicated to
My Wife Madhu

Preface

Having served in the Planning Commission for nearly five years—as Joint Secretary (State Plans) (1985-86) and then as Advisor (State Plans) (1989-92)—I had been taken a back to learn that the sixty-five years old institution had suddenly been abolished being replaced by a new institution NITI Aayog on the 1st January, 2015. Nearly four years have since elapsed. This is an attempt to briefly analyse some aspects of this new institution, how it has been functioning and its contribution in these initial years of its existence.

I am grateful to my wife Madhu for suggesting to me and encouraging and helping me to write this small book.

Our sons Yujush and Rishabh greatly helped me in this endeavour. I gratefully acknowledge this.

K.D. Saksena

Contents

Annexures

1
Abolition of Union Planning Commission and Advent of NITI Aayog in India

In his speech on August 15, 2014, the Prime Minister announced that "within a short period we will replace the Planning Commission with a new institution, having a new design and structure ....to promote the aspirations of state governments seeking development, to empower the state governments, and to empower the federal structure" (Annexure 1). Underlying this announcement is a very strong indictment of the functioning of the Union Planning Commission over the last sixty-five years by its present Chairman, the Prime Minister himself, before the nation, which may raise questions such as follows:

(a) What exactly has been so fundamentally wrong with the functioning of the Planning Commission in its dealings with the States which necessitated its immediate replacement by another organisation?

(b) 'Economic and social planning' is at serial no. 20 of List (III)—Concurrent List in the Seventh Schedule; and as per Article 246(2) of the Constitution, both Parliament and the Legislature of any State have power to make laws with respect to any of the matters enumerated in the Concurrent List. States generally have their own Planning Commissions/Boards and have been making and implementing their own plans without any hindrance from the Union Planning Commission. In view of this position, how the states and the federal structure are now to be further empowered by abolishing Union Planning Commission itself and creating NITI Aayog in its place, has not been indicated.

2. In his "opening remarks at the consultation meeting with CMs on 07 Dec., 2014, the Prime Minister" stressed the need for a suitable body to replace the Planning Commission (Annexure 2), so that the strengths of the country can be suitably harnessed. He further said that as Chief Minister of Gujarat he had been attending meetings of the Planning Commission "and had felt the need for a better platform to articulate the views of the states", and a new mechanism to deliver growth and development". He further said that "states should have a key role in the new body to replace the Planning Commission", and there should be an effective mechanism to address inter-state disputes. To "set the tone for the discussion", the Prime Minister (P.M.) asked: "Can we develop a new mechanism that plans according to India's strengths, empowers states, and brings on board all economic activity including that which happens outside the Government" (Annexure 2).

3. Summing up, the P.M. said that the new body to replace the Planning Commission should be able to:

(a) suitably harness the strengths of the country;
(b) provide a better platform to articulate the views of the States;
(c) enable the States to play a key role in the new body;
(d) provide an effective mechanism to address inter-state disputes; and
(e) provide a new mechanism that plans according to India's strengths, and in the process empowers the States, bringing on board all economic activity including that which happens outside the Government (Annexure 4).

4. It may be pointed out here that for inter-state disputes, we already have a constitutional mechanism—the Inter State Council set up under Article 263 of the Constitution.

5. The now abolished Planning Commission was in fact the "mechanism that planned" according to developmental needs and the resources which could be mobilised. But in regard to activities outside the Government, its role was generally indicative only. The Five Year and Annual Plans of the Central and State Governments did actually harness the resources of the Centre and the States for the development of the country, and several States played a key role in this endeavour.

For economic activity outside the plan in the private sector, the planning had been only indicative.

6. On the 1st January, 2015, the country learnt that the 65 years old Planning Commission, which gave the country twelve Five Years Plans carefully assessing and mobilising resources—monetary and material—for nation building and raising the levels of living of the people—has been abolished and replaced by a new institution called 'National Institution for Transforming India' or NITI Aayog "set up as a 'Think Tank' of the Government—a directional and policy dynamo .... to provide governments at the Central and State levels strategic and technical advice across the spectrum of key elements of policy. This includes the matters of national and international import on the economic front, dissemination of best practices from within the country as well as from other nations, the infusion of new policy ideas and specific issue–based support." With this description, the addition of the word "Aayog" appears to be unnecessary, as it makes it an institution and a commission (आयोग) simultaneously (Annexure 3).

7. The reasons for replacing the Planning Commission by NITI Aayog given in the Cabinet Resolution dated 01 January, 2015 are somewhat strange and totally unconvincing. While acknowledging the Planning Commission's role in the country being transformed from "an underdeveloped economy" to an "emergent global nation with one of the world's largest economies," it is argued that the "one-size fits-all" approach inherent in central planning, has the potential of creating needless tensions and undermining the harmony needed for national effort."

8. There is no basis for the statement that the Planning Commission had been an instrument of central planning. There has always been decentralised and multi-level planning in India at the village Panchayat, Block, District, State and Central levels, based on the felt needs, priorities and resources mobilisation at each of these levels. Centralised planning could be done only in centralised command economies like the former USSR or China. India has, and always had, decentralised and democratic planning at each level, as indicated above.

9. Similarly, there has never been "one-size fits all" approach to

planning at any level in India, there being as many different sizes and contents of plans at various levels as there are villages, Panchayats, Blocks, Districts and States, depending on their respective perceptions of their felt needs, priorities and resources which could be mobilised. There is ample documentary evidence to prove this.

10. The Cabinet Resolution dated the 1st January, 2015 is not a clear, concise, crisp yet comprehensive document like the earlier and now superceded document dated the 15th March, 1950 (Annexure 4). It is a free flowing and rambling script touching, generally superficially, several unrelated or loosely related issues/ideas culminating in setting up an institution which is supposed to partake the character of both an institution and a commission to do several difficult and sometimes unrelated things simultaneously, and generally within an indefinite time-frame.

11. The new Resolution first identifies the forces transforming India which include:

(a) "The industry and services sectors which have developed and are operating on a global scale now";
(b) "India's traditional strength in agriculture" and "the need to continue to improve, and move from pure food security to a focus on a mix of agricultural production as well as the actual returns that farmers get from their produce";
(c) India needs to be an active player in the debates and deliberations on the global commons, especially in unchartered areas;
(d) The need to ensure that India's middle class, which "has been an important driver of growth" remains engaged and its potential is fully realised";
(e) "India's pool of entrepreneurial, scientific and intellectual human capital" "needs to be leveraged through appropriate policy initiatives";
(f) The NRI's "spread across more than 200 countries" are a significant geo-economic and geo-political strength" and "future national policies must incorporate this strength in order to broaden their participation in the new India beyond just financial support";

(g) Urbanisation needs to be made "an integral part of our policy for development"; and
(h) "Government and governance have to be conducted in an environment of total transparency-using technology to reduce opacity and thereby, the potential for misadventures in governing".

12. The new Resolution also says that "our development model has to become more consensual and co-operative. It must embrace the specific demands of states, regions and localities. A shared vision of national development has to be worked out based on human dignity, national self-respect and an inclusive and sustainable development path".

13. The new Resolution then mentions the challengers facing the country "which have also become more complex":

(a) India's demographic dividend has to be leveraged fruitfully through education, skill development, elimination of gender bias, and employment".
(b) Poverty elimination and giving every Indian an opportunity to live a life of dignity and self-respect.
(c) 'Antyodaya'–the goal being ensuring that the poorest of the poor get the benefit of development.
(d) Villages "need to be fully integrated institutionally into the developmental process."
(e) India has more than 50 million small businesses, which are a major source of employment creation. "Policy making must focus on providing necessary support to this sector in terms of skill and knowledge upgrades and access to financial capital and relevant technology."
(f) Environmentally sound development. Each element of our environment, namely water, land and forest, must be protected in a manner that takes into account their inter-linkages with climate and people so as to ensure that development does not sully the quality of life of the present and future generations".

14. "Government will continue to set policies that anticipate and reflect the country's requirements, and execute them in a just manner for the benefit of the citizens". "In the context of governance structures" there is "need for setting up an institution that serves as a Think Tank

of the Government—a directional and policy dynamo which has to provide governments at the central and state levels with relevant strategic and technical advice across the spectrum of key elements of policy. This includes matters of national and international import on the economic front, dissemination of best practices from within the country as well as from other nations, the infusion of new policy ideas and specific issue-based support". "An important evolutionary change from the past will be replacing centre to state one way flow of policy to a genuine and continuing partnership with the states." "While incorporating positive influences from the world, the new institution has to zero in on what will work in and for India. It will be a Bharatiya approach to development."

15. The NITI Aayog will work towards the following objectives:

"(a)To evolve a shared vision of national development priorities, sectors and strategies with the active involvement of states in the light of national objectives. The vision of NITI Aayog will then provide a framework national agenda for the Prime Minister and the Chief Minister to provide impetus to.

(b) To foster co-operative federalism through structured support initiatives and mechanisms with the states on a continuous basis, recognising that strong states make a strong nation.

(c) To develop mechanisms to formulate credible plans at the village level and aggregate them progressively at higher levels of government.

(d) To ensure, on areas that are specifically referred to it, that the interests of national security are incorporated in economic strategy and policy.

(e) To pay special attention to the sections of our society that may be at risk of not benefitting adequately from economic progress.

(f) To design strategic and long term policy and programme frameworks and initiatives, and monitor their progress and their efficacy. The lessons learnt through monitoring and feedback will be used for making innovative improvement, including mid-course corrections.

(g) To provide advice and encourage partnership between key stakeholders and national and international like minded Think Tanks, as well as educational and policy research institutions.

(h) To create a knowledge, innovations and entrepreneurial support system through a collaborative community of national and international experts, practitioners and other partners.

(i) To offer a platform for resolution of inter-sectoral and inter-departmental issues in order to accelerate the implementation of the development agenda.

(j) To maintain a state-of-the-art Resource Centre, be a repository of research on good governance and best practices in sustainable and equitable development as well as help their dissemination to stakeholders.

(k) To actively monitor and evaluate the implementation of programme and initiatives, including the identification of needed resources so as to strengthen the probability of success and scope of delivery.

(l) To focus on technology upgradation and capacity building for implementation of programmes and initiatives.

(m) To undertake other activities as may necessary in order to further the execution of the national development agenda, and the objectives mentioned above."

16. The organisational structure of the NITI Aayog will be as follows:

(a) Prime Minister of India will be the Chairperson.

(b) Governing Council comprising the Chief Ministers of all the States and Lt. Governors of Union Territories

(c) Regional Councils to be formed to address specific issues and contingencies impacting more than one State or a region for a specified term. The Regional Councils will be convened by the Prime Minister, and will consist of the Chief Ministers of States and Lt. Governors of UTs, to be chaired by the Prime Minister or his nominee.

(d) Experts, specialists and practitioners with relevant domain knowledge as special invitees to be nominated by the Prime Minister.

Full-time Organisational Framework

Chairperson:	Prime Minister Vice-Chairpersons to be appointed by the Prime Minister
Members:	Full time
Ex-officio Members:	Maximum 4 from the Union Council of Ministers to be nominated by the P.M.

Part-time Members:	Maximum 2 from leading universities and research organisations and other relevant institutions in an ex-officio capacity on a rotational basis.
Chief Executive Officer:	To be appointed by the P.M. for a fixed tenure in the rank of Secretary to Govt. of India.

Secretariat as deemed necessary

"Through its commitment to a co-operative federalism, promotion of citizen engagement, egalitarian access to opportunity, participative and adaptive governance and increasing use of technology, the NITI Aayog will seek to provide a critical directional and strategic input into the development process. This, along with being the incubator of ideas for development, will be the core mission of NITI Aayog."

17. The now abolished National Development Council was not a part of the then existing Planning Commission, but a separate institution, independent of and higher than, the Planning Commission, whose approval had to be obtained by the Planning Commission on all vital matters like the Approach Paper, and the 'Five Year Plan' documents after their being considered and cleared by the Union Cabinet. It is only after NDC's approval that these documents were submitted to both houses of the Parliament. The Chief Ministers, who used to be the members of the then existing NDC, have now become Members of NITI Aayog's Governing Body headed by the Prime Minister, and have thus ceased to be part of a separate, independent and superior body like the now abolished NDC. There is now virtual supremacy of the Prime Minister heading the Governing Body, and the Prime Minister's Office, which is not conducive to cooperative federalism.

18. Though similarly constituted, NITI Aayog, with a large number of Advisers of different ranks and categories, huge research, administrative, clerical and other staff, consultants, etc., neither prepares any draft plan, nor has to monitor anything. It may possibly be providing some research and secretariat assistance required in the preparation of the 'Three Years Agenda', 'Seven Years Strategy' and 'Fifteen Years Vision' documents and related papers. It appears to be

functioning more or less like a subordinate office of the PMO, or an extension of the PMO, deriving power and authority from it, and not as an independent body of professionals with experience and expertise in different areas and disciplines.

19. It is pertinent to point out here that the Aayog has collected information, data and views/opinion from hundreds of outside consultants, professionals and experts for preparing the "Three Years Agenda", spending a lot of money and time, which may not be implementable unless a realistic assessment of the funds required for implementing it are carefully worked out, and sources from which the required funds could be mobilised and made available to the implementing agencies as per their requirements identified, and the progress of implementation is monitored and reviewed on a regular basis.

20. A note dated 22 April, 2017 captioned "Significant Achievements of NITI Aayog Over the Last Three Years" highlights, inter-alia, the following facts (Annexure 5):

(i) The NITI Aayog, which has the strength of Members, Advisers, and Secretariat staff comparable to the erstwhile Union Planning Commission has done practically very little work in the nearly four years of its existence. In most of the cases, the work reported to have been done by it could have as well been done by the concerned Ministries to the extent it was considered feasible or necessary; and a separate Aayog may not be required for doing it.

(ii) The "3-Years Action Agenda" prepared by the Aayog is a meaningless exercise in the absence of year-wise break-up of monitorable targets to be achieved, the modalities for implementation and assessment and mobilisation of the funds required.

(iii) In almost all other cases, the work reported to have been done appears to be unnecessary duplication or repetition of the work of the concerned Ministry or Department of the Government.

(iv) There has hardly been any evidence as yet of the Aayog being a policy dynamo or its providing "a critical directional and strategic input into the development process", as envisaged.

21. The excerpts from the speech of the Prime Minister on August 15, 2014 at Annexure 1 do not give any indication whether the momentous decision to abolish a sixty-five years old institution like the Planning Commission had been taken by the Government on the basis of any consensus arrived at after discussion at any forum like the Consultative Committee of the Ministry of Planning, or National Development Council or Inter State Council (with whom the recommendations of the Sarkaria Commission relating to the Planning Commission had been under consideration), or the Parliament. There is also no indication of any communication being sent to the Chief Ministers by the P.M. or from any other appropriate authority explaining the proposal and its implications; and the responses received from them being duly considered by the P.M. and the Cabinet. A RTI query dated May 1, 2015 by the author seeking information specifically on such points remained unanswered. It appears that some brainstorming sessions were held on such issues with some Chief Ministers and others after the PM's above announcement, which were meaningless sham shows and an afterthought to cover up a patently undemocratic act.

2

Nehru's Planning Model Vs. Modi's Transformation Model

Nehru's model for India's development, if at all we can call it so, as briefly spelt out in the Govt. of India's Cabinet Resolution dated the 15th March, 1950 setting up the Planning Commission (Annexure 4) is based on his perception of economic realities at that time, and the proposition that mobilisation of real and monetary resources required is essential for initiating and sustaining any development or planning process. The Resolution briefly mentions the major problems the country had been facing at that time, such as, "the absence of adequate coordination and of sufficiently precise information about the availability of resources"; the emergence of new geographical and economic facts with the integration of former Indian States with the rest of the country; and "the need for a fresh assessment of the financial and other resources". "These factors highlighted the need for comprehensive planning based on careful assessment of resources and an objective analysis of all the relevant economic factors."

2. It is pertinent to point out that para 3 of this Resolution says that the planning exercise has to be carried out bearing is mind that "the Constitution of India has guaranteed certain fundamental rights to the citizens of India and enunciated certain directive principles of state policy, in particular, that the state shall strive to promote the welfare of the people by securing and protecting as effectively as it may, a social order in which justice, social, economic and political, shall inform all the institutions of the national life and shall direct its policy towards securing the welfare of the people by seeking, among other things:

"(a) that the citizens, men and women, equally, have the right to an adequate means of livelihood;
(b) that the ownership and control of the material resources of the community are so distributed as best to subserve the common good; and
(c) that the operation of the economic system does not result in the concentration of wealth and means of production to the common detriment."

3. The Resolution further says that "having regard to these rights and in furtherance of these principles as well as the declared objective of the government to promote a rapid rise in the standard of living of the people by efficient exploitation of the resources of the country, increasing production, and offering opportunities to all for employment in the service of the community", the Planning Commission will formulate a plan for the effective and balanced utilization of the country's resources".

4. The resolution then states, in an absolutely clear and concise manner the essential steps involved in the planning process, and the composition of the Planning Commission.

4.1. The above resolution is a clear and concise statement of the action required to be taken for comprehensive planning in a developing country like India with practically no political overtones. The objectives sought to be achieved are similarly free from any political bias, and based on provisions of the Constitution of India. That is why there has been no tampering with the planning process outlined in this resolution, and the Twelve Five Year Plans and Annual Plans formulated and implemented during the period 1950-51 to 2016-17 broadly conformed to the process outlined in this resolution.

4.2. Planning Commission was set up in pursuance of entry at Serial No. 20 of List 111—Concurrent List: Economic and Social Planning, of the Constitution of India. The resolution also mentions the following reasons for "the appointment of a Planning Commission":

(i) Need for "adequate coordination and of sufficiently precise information about the availability of resources."
(ii) "Need for comprehensive planning based on a careful appraisal of resources and an objective analysis of all relevant economic factors."

(iii) Directive Principles of State Policy, particularly "that the state shall strive to promote the welfare of the people by securing and protecting as effectively as it may a social order in which justice, social, economic and political shall inform all the institutions of national life and shall direct the policy towards securing" these objectives.

4.3 This Resolution further states "that in such social order all citizens", men and women equally have the right to an adequate means of livelihood;" "ownership and control of the material resources of the community are so distributed as best to subserve the common good;" and the operation of the economic system does not result in the concentration of wealth and means of production to the common detriment."

4.4 The Resolution thus states clearly, precisely and comprehensively what may be described as the essence of the planning process in a democracy anywhere anytime; and is absolutely incontrovertible. It is based on, and it refers to the relevant provisions of the Constitution, and not to any saying of any political or spiritual leader.

4.5 The above Resolution is a brief statement of the action required to be taken for comprehensive planning in a developing country like India with practically no political overtones. The objectives sought to be achieved are similarly free from any political bias, and based on express provisions of the Constitution of India. That is why there has been no tampering with the planning process outlined is this Resolution, and the Twelve Five Year Plans formulated and implemented during the years 1950-51 to 2016-17 broadly conformed to the processes and principles outlined in this Resolution.

5. Modi's model, as elaborately stated in the Cabinet Resolution dated the 1st January, 2015 (Annexure 3), briefly stated, is as follows:

5.1. In the first five paragraphs, this resolution mentions several facts, some obvious and some controversial, which have transformed India. In para 6 again, some other forces transforming India have been indicated. Para 7 states how "technology and access to information have accentuated the unity and diversity that define us". Para 8 states some of the "challenges we face as country", e.g. leveraging "demographic dividend", "poverty elimination", 'Antyodaya' and environmentally sound development.

6. Para 9 of this Resolution mentions the 'pillars' on which the "effective governance in India will rest on", such as "pro-people agenda that fulfills the aspirations of the society as well as the individual", "empowering women", "equality of opportunity to our country's youth", "transparency through the use of technology", etc.

7. The resolution concludes that the changed requirements of our country point to the need for setting up an institution that serves as a Think Tank of the government—a directional and policy dynamo, which "has to provide governments at the central and state levels with relevant strategic and technical advice across the spectrum of key elements of policy". "This includes matters of national and international import on the economic front, dissemination of best practices from within the country as well as from other nations, the infusion of new policy ideas and specific issues based support. The institution has to be able to respond to the changing and more integrated world that India is part of."

8. The January 2015 Resolution clearly and comprehensively discards the concepts of planning and planned development. While the March 1950 Resolution led to the preparation and implementation of development plans based on joint assessment of financial and real resources, felt needs and short-term and long-term social and economic objectives, both by the Central Ministries and the States, the January 2015 Resolution, while abolishing the Union Planning Commission, and creating NITI Aayog, abolished planning and planned development at the Central Govt. level, while it continues at the states and lower levels as before. At the national level, the NITI Aayog has prepared a Three Year Agenda of Development, the year-wise break-up and the sources of funding which are not known. There has also been practically no participation of the Central Ministries in the preparation of this Agenda, although its contents relate to several Central Ministries and Departments. The Central Ministries may not feel bound by this Agenda as they have not been associated with its preparation or finalisation, but they may still have to fall in line if the Prime Minister's Office so directs. How this Agenda would be implemented and monitored, and how it would transform India, only future may tell.

9. Our Finance Minister, Shri Arun Jaitley's remarks in this regard are interesting and thought provoking. He is reported to have observed: "The 65 years old Planning Commission had become a redundant organisation. It was relevant in a command economy, but not any longer. India is a diversified country and its states are in various phases

of economic development along with their own strengths and weaknesses. In this context 'a one size fits all' approach to economic development is obsolete. It cannot make India competitive in today's global economy."

10. India neither is, nor has ever been, a planned economy, or a command economy.

10.1. A planned economy is the one is which production, prices, income, etc. are determined centrally by Government.

10.2. Command economy is also a planned economy in which crucial economic processes are determined largely not by market forces, but an economic planning body, which implements society's major economic goals. In such a system, the greater part of production activity is determined by obligatory output and input targets generated by vertical signals from one administrative hierarchical body.

10.3. Indian economy can appropriately be described as a mixed economy in which both private sector and public sector co-exist and co-operate and compete with each other, depending on market conditions as well as Government policy at any particular time. It is basically a market economy in which prices and production are determined not by the Government or any Central authority but by market forces of demand and supply, and technological conditions or constraints. The erstwhile Planning Commission in its entire sixty-five years life did not at all interfere with the free play of market forces in determining prices or production or distribution of goods and services, which had all been market determined: it only facilitated both the pubic and private sectors to freely operate in a complimentary and co-operative manner to maximize production and minimize costs, and put the economy on a higher growth trajectory ensuring, to the extent practicable, equitable sharing of the fruits of growth by all sections of the population.

10.4. It would be both unreasonable and unfair to hold planning or Planning Commission responsible for the regulations and restrictions on production and imports, which were partly statutory and partly the result of the economic policies of the Government based on their perception of economic realities at that time. Such restrictions had been relaxed in stages facilitating inter-alia, the flow of foreign capital and technology which significantly contributed to growth and development of both industry and agriculture. Planning Commission took cognizance of this change in economic environment and contributed to the acceleration of this change through plans and planning mechanisms.

11. It is thus utterly wrong and misleading to say that there had ever been a command economy in the post-independence India. India has all along been, and still is, a market economy (except very few strategic areas being reserved for the public sector). By and large, the market forces determine prices and the allocation of resources; and Government regulates these generally through its monetary and fiscal policies. Planning in India has all along been indicative in nature, making a realistic assessment of resources which could be mobilised, deciding national priorities and indicating the allocation of resources necessary for achieving the targetted GDP growth rate and other socio-economic objectives. The entire process of planning has been democratic involving public debate on all vital economic issues, participation of states (which have their own planning bodies) and evolving a national consensus through open discussion in the meetings of the institutions like the Union Planning Commission and the National Development Council (which included Chief Ministers of the States) and allowing full freedom to the states within the constitutional framework of a federal polity. The development plans of Central Ministries and States formulated and finalised through this open and democratic process according to the shared vision and perceptions of representatives of the States and the Centre could never be the same for all; and there could possibly be no question of there being any imposition of any one size or pattern on all States or Central Ministries in development plans prepared and finalised through such process; and the maxim 'one size fits all' is, and has always been totally irrelevant and inapplicable to plans formulated and finalised by an open democratic process out-lined above.

12. The following observations made in Chapter 1 "Objectives and Orientation" of the Eighth Five Year Plan, which too explain the position on this point, are reproduced below:

"When the term "planning" was, for the first time officially defined in the First Five Year Plan document, the term used was "democratic planning" as distinct from a "plan based on regimentation". The centralised planning of the type practised in socialist economies did not exist in India, ever. In practice, the market has determined allocations in a major segment of the economy. As a corollary to this, the role of Planning Commission needs to be redefined. It has to play an integrative role in developing a holistic approach to the policy formulation in critical and inter-sectoral areas of human and economic development. Planning in our country still has a large role to play.

Planning is needed for creating social infrastructure and for human development. We need to build schools, hospitals and institutions of excellence and scientific research. We have to plan and structure the system of education to cultivate necessary culture, skills and value systems..."

13. It is pertinent to quote the observations of two former Prime Ministers relating to the need and relevance of developmental planning in India in the above context.

13.1. In his foreword to the Eighth Plan, Prime Minister Shri P.V. Narasimha Rao observed as follows:

> "Planning has been one of the pillars of our policies since independence. There is today a recognition that in many areas development can best be ensured by freeing them of unnecessary controls and regulations and withdrawing state intervention. At the same time we believe that growth and development of the country cannot be left entirely to the market mechanism. The market can be expected to bring about an "equilibrium" between demand backed by purchasing power and "supply", but it will not be able to ensure a balance between "need" and supply. Planning is necessary to overcome such limitations of the market mechanism. Planning is necessary for macro-economic management, for taking care of the poor and the downtrodden, who are mostly outside the market system and have little asset endowment. It is thus not a choice between market mechanism and planning; the challenge is to effectively dovetail the two so that they are complementary to each other."
>
> Let us dedicate ourselves to the task of achieving the objectives set for the plan. Let us together build an India that is vibrant and modern; and an India that is socially integrated and economically strong."

13.2. Subsequently, in the foreword to the Tenth Plan, Shri Atal Bihari Vajpayee made the following observations:

> "Planning has been one of the pillars to our approach to economic development since independence and has stood us is good stead. Planning is not a static concept, and each of our plans has reflected the changing imperatives of the times.

While working out the road map we need to follow my vision of doubling the per capita income of our country and providing one crore opportunities in the next ten years, the Planning Commission has firmly kept in view the ongoing process of transition to a market economy"... The changing role of the Government and its relationship with the private sector forms the cornerstone of the Plan.

The unanimous adoption of the Tenth Five Year Plan by the National Development Council is a confirmation of our collective belief in the potential of our country and the extent to which we share a common vision of the future. I congratulate the Deputy Chairman, Members and officials of the Planning Commission for having done a commendable job in shaping and giving substance to this shared vision...."

3

NITI Aayog: Their Agenda and Staff

As mentioned earlier, the Prime Minister had announced on August 15, 2014 itself that the Planning Commission will shortly be replaced by "a new institution, having a new design and structure to promote the aspirations of the State Governments seeking development, to empower the State Governments and to empower the federal structure." (Annexure 1). This was followed by his talking the Chief Ministers on 07.12.2014 in a consultation meeting with them that there is need for a suitable body to replace the Planning Commissions for—

(a) suitably harnessing the strength of the country;
(b) providing a better platform to articulate the views of the States; and
(c) a new mechanism to deliver growth and development in which the States have a key role (Annexure 2).

2. It is not clear what exactly are being considered as "strength of the country" and what is meant by "suitably harnessing" them. It could possibly mean 'human resources' or 'scientific and technical personnel', or availability of some natural resources or some goods or services which could be exported and thereby enable the country to earn valuable foreign exchange, or some exportable information technology and skills.

2.1. In the planning process before the abolition of the Planning Commission, the States did have a very important role. In the "New mechanism to deliver growth and development" the P.M. has in mind now, how would that role change, has not been spelt out.

3. There has been no indication of anything else happening in this regard between 15.08.2014 and 07.12.2014 or thereafter till the New Year's day dated 01.01.2015, when the nation learnt that the 65 years old Planning Commission, which had been playing a key role in transforming India from an underdeveloped and predominantly backward agrarian and industrial economy into one of the major industrial powers, has indeed been abolished, and replaced by NITI Aayog—a seemingly illogical name, being an 'institution' and a 'commission' (Aayog) simultaneously. However, on a little reflection, it became clear that besides having an illogical name, it is an altogether different institution in its constitution, functions and role. It has nothing to do with formulation of plans "for the most effective and balanced utilisation of the country's resources." It is not at all a planning body, has nothing to do with any assessment of resources available or which could be mobilised for investment; nor does it examine and approve after discussion any development plan or its mode of financing. It is not designed to harness strengths of the country or provide a platform for the states to articulate their views, but it prepares an 'agenda' for development without indicating precisely the implementing agency, the funds required and the sources from which they could be mobilised (Annexure 6).

4. The momentous decision of abolishing on the 1st January, 2015, a sixty-five years old institution, which had undeniably played an important role in transforming a relatively poor, agrarian economy into an agriculturally as well as industrially developed, self-reliant economy, and one of the major economic powers internationally, and replacing it with a new institution called NITI Aayog, both surprised and shocked the country. An important question which would strike anyone would be as to what exactly had gone so seriously and irremediably wrong with the then existing Planning Commission necessitating such swift and sudden action, which might change the nature and course of the Indian economy in the years to come. It may not be easy to find an answer, which only time may tell.

5. A relatively easier question which may arise is: has any committee or commission examined the working of the now abolished Planning Commission whose report had been still under consideration by a constitutional body called the Inter-State Council; and such decision has been taken and implemented without waiting for its findings or report?

6. Yet another question, which might be bothering some even now is whether a proper democratic procedure of consideration and decision-making had been followed while taking such a historic decision, which may have far reaching consequences. Specifically, whether the rationale for abolishing a national institution like the erstwhile Planning Commission been properly projected to the institutions like the National Development Council (before abolishing the NDC itself) the Inter State Council (before whom the Sarkaria Commission's recommendations relating to the Planning Commission were still under consideration); the Consultative Committee of the Ministry of Planning and the Parliament itself? Whether the Prime Minister had written to the Chief Ministers explaining the proposal and its rationale and the responses received properly processed and considered. Persistent efforts made by the author to obtain such relevant information under the Right to Information Act, 2005 have not succeeded so far.

7. It may be mentioned here that the Three Year Action Agenda has been published by NITI Aayog on 1 August, 2017 recommending policy changes and programmes for action for the period without holding any prior consultations/discussions with the concerned States and the representative bodies mentioned above. The policy and other recommendations have presumably been made on the basis of written inputs from about 94 experts and consultation with more than 260 other experts in addition to the experts available in the Aayog itself.

7.1 The Three Year Agenda is co-terminus with the term of the Fourteenth Finance Commission award period.

8. There appears to be no logic for the termination of Three Year Agenda by the end of the 14th Finance Commission award period. Finance Commission is set up according to Article 280 of the Constitution every five years for recommending devolution of tax revenues to the States. It prepares forecasts of the revenue receipts and expenditure of the State Governments and recommends grants against financial gaps of those states which have deficits even after devolution of Central Taxes.

9. The Central Assistance for State Plans is given for the States' Annual Plans according to a formula known as Gadgil-Mukherjee Formula (1991) additionally and independently of any other financial assistance.

10. The very first para of the Preface to the three years Action Agenda eloquently describes its present position and predicament (Annexure 6):

> "On 1st January, 2015, the National Institution for Transforming India or NITI Aayog came into existence as the government's premier Think Tank. Subsequently, vide Office Order No. PMO ID No. 360/31/C/38/2014–ES-11 dated 09.05.2016…., the Prime Minister's Office advised NITI Aayog to prepare Fifteen Year Vision, Seven Year Strategy and Three Year Action Agenda documents.... Accordingly the present document is being published to recommend policy changes and programme for action from 2017-18 to 2019-20, the last three years of the Fourteenth Finance Commission. A second document containing the Fifteen Years Vision and Seven Years Strategy is currently under preparation at the NITI Aayog."

11. It may be mentioned here that the Three Year Action Agenda (2017-18 to 2019-20) is published by NITI Aayog on 1 August, 2017 recommending policy changes and programmes for action for this three years period. This document, however, does not indicate: (i) the 'Action Points' for the concerned states (indicating the names of the states); (ii) requirements and availability of funds; (iii) realistic time-frame for completing action as envisaged; (iv) the implementing agency for each action point, and (v) year-wise break-ups, without which the Action Agenda may remain on paper only (Annexure 6).

12. A copy of the PMO's letter dated 09.05.2016 referred to above is at Annexure 7. This letter outlines the status and mode of functioning of NITI Aayog as compared to its predecessor Union Planning Commission and its implications, which may be stated as follows:

(i) The erstwhile Union Planning Commission was an independent body which took orders from only the National Development Council or the Parliament, and not from the PMO or any other Government office of any Ministry or Government Department.

(ii) With the abolition of the Union Planning Commission and the 'Plans' prepared or approved by it, the terms like "plan" and "non-plan" have, in any case, been rendered meaningless. Ministry of Finance have accordingly decided to do away with them from the year 2017-18 and closely work with the State Finance Department to align Central and State Budgets in the matter.

(iii) Any "planning cycle", which would now mean "action agenda", should now factor in periodicity of Finance Commission's" recommendations and political mandate (5 years of Government). However, as the years and dates of holding General Elections to the State Assemblies may be different, their could be overlapping. Whether it would create any problems, may need to be examined.

(iv) Five Year Plans would be discontinued after the 12th Five Year Plan. It is not clear whether Central Ministries, which so far had their own Five Year Plans, would now be required by the PMO or the Finance Ministry to discontinue the practice of having Five Year and Annual Plans of their own and fall in line. The states generally have their own State Planning Commissions or State Planning Boards and frame their own Five Year and Annual Plans. Whether this would pose any problems of coordination and funding of these plans may need to be examined.

(v) The practice of formulating Five Year Plans for the country would be discontinued after the 12th Five Year Plan. Thereafter, first a longer vision of 15 years may be formulated keeping in view the social goals set and/or proposed and Sustainable Social Development Goals (Annexure 8). To convert this longer vision into implementable policy and action, a seven years strategy from 2017-18 may be formulated as part of a "National Development Agenda" with a mid-term review after three years. The three years time-frame would be aligned to predictability of financial resources during the 14th Finance Commission Award period. This will also help translating into action the goals of the government to be achieved by 2019.

(vi) The National Development Agenda should go beyond the traditional area of 'Plan' and cover the aspects of Internal Security, Defence, etc. as well, and may be prepared by NITI Aayog.

13. Besides a statement showing seventeen Sustainable Development Goals (SDGs) (Annexure 8), a news item captioned "Government reduces number of centrally sponsored schemes to 28"

in the Economic Times (updated APR 10, 2017) with an 'Expenditure Profile 2018-2019' enclosed with it is at Annexure 9. The available information does not indicate the pattern of funding by the centre and the states, and how the progress would be monitored so as to achieve the targets set, and ensure required remedial action (Annexure 9).

13.1. It may neither be feasible nor desirable to include Internal Security, Defence, etc. in the document prepared by NITI Aayog. These are Confidential/Secret, classified documents, and papers relating to them may need to be kept separate and away from Government Department/Agencies other than those given the responsibility of keeping and using them as and when needed. Necessary guidance in this regard would need to be given by the concerned Ministry or organisation of the Government of India. The matter may also need to be taken up and discussed with the PMO at appropriate level.

14. Organisational Set-up of NITI Aayog

NITI Aayog functions through the Team India Hub (TIH) and Knowledge and Innovation Hub (KIH), each headed by an Additional Secretary. The newly created vertical units under TIH and KIH are as under (as per the OUTCOME BUDGET, 2016-17 of NITI):

14.1. Vertical Units

(i) Agriculture
(ii) Rural Development
(iii) Industry (including Textiles, Handlooms, Handicrafts and MSMI)
(iv) International Trade
(v) Infrastructure (I)–Digital Connectivity Including Rural Connectivity
(vi) Infrastructure (II)–Energy and Climate Change
(vii) Infrastructure (III) –Physical Connectivity
(viii) Infrastructure with other Division, Project Monitoring including E-Samiksha, Project Monitoring Group (PMG), Pro-Active Governance and Timely Implementation (PRAGATI) and On-line Computerised Monitoring System (OCMS), etc.
(ix) Pradhan Mantri Gram Sadak Yojna (PMGSY)
(x) Science and Technology, Innovation, R&D
(xi) Social Justice
(xii) Natural Resources and Environment
(xiii) Data Management and Analysis

(xiv) Macro-economics
(xv) Special Studies (including special reference regarding interests of National Security in Economic Strategy and Policy)
(xvi) Health, Nutrition, Women and Children
(xvii) Managing Urbanisation
(xviii) Education
(xix) Skill Development & Employment
(xx) District and Village Level Plans
(xxi) Governance and Public Service Delivery

14.2. Core Divisions

(i) Administration (including GA)
(ii) Governing Council Secretariat (including coordination with PMs/Cab. Sectt.)
(iii) PIB/Public Private Partnership Appraisal Committee (PPAC) and Programme Appraisal Secretariat
(iv) Financial Resources (including matters pertaining to State Finance and Union Budgets)
(v) Research and Study Scheme
(vi) Parliament, RTI and Official Language
(vii) Communication and Publications
- National Institute for Labour Economic Research & Development (NILRED) (Formerly Institution of Applied Manpower Research-IAMR) which is an autonomous institution. Its primary objectives include research, data collection, and education and training in all aspects of Human Capital Planning and Human Resource Development.
- Development Monitoring and Evaluation Office (DMEO) has been constituted on 18 September, 2015 by merging the Programme Evaluation Organisation (PEO) and the Independent Evaluation Office (IEO); and notified as an attached office under the aegis of NITI for fulfilling the mandate of evaluation and monitoring assigned to NITI Aayog.

14.3. The fact that the administrative head of NITI Aayog is a Chief Executive Officer (CEO) and not a Secretary to Government of India may signal severing of any direct relations of the Aayog with any Ministry except the Ministry of Planning; and may indicate its functioning more or less as an extension of the Prime Minister's Office (PMO), Prime Minister being its Chairman. As the NITI Aayog has nothing to do with the approval or financing of the State Plans now, the Aayog may have practically no clout or contact with any State Government except by way of conveying or carrying out Prime Minister's ideas or instructions. The Aayog may not be considered to be an independent body of experts by the states, familiar with the problems relating to development of the states.

14.4. Considering that unlike its predecessor (now defunct Planning Commission), the NITI Aayog has practically no role in—

(a) formulation, implementation, monitoring, review and taking necessary remedial action in the case of State Plans and the plans of the Central Ministries; and
(b) aiding and advising the States and the Central Ministries in matters relating to large public investments or policies of the States and the Central Government.

The numerous divisions with teams of Advisers of different disciplines with complimentary research and other staff appear to the unnecessary; and need to be suitably scaled down after careful consideration. NITI Aayog at present appears to be more heavily manned than its predecessor, which had been required to do much more work.

4
Objectives of NITI Aayog

Para 12 of the Cabinet Resolution setting up the NITI Aayog (Annexure 3) states thirteen objectives (a. to m.) for which NITI Aayog will work which have been "proposed after extensive consultation across the spectrum of stakeholders including inter-alia, state governments, domain experts and relevant institutions". Nearly four years have since elapsed—a long enough period to register perceptible progress in the achievement of these objectives. A brief stock taking exercise could justifiably be done at this stage which could possibly give indications of the progress made in the first four years and likely to be made further in the years to become to register and maintain the desired pace of progress.

2. The first objective of NITI Aayog as stated in the Cabinet Resolution dated 01.01.2015 (Annexure 3) setting up this institution is as follows:

> "To evolve a shared vision of national development priorities, sectors and strategies with the active involvement of states in the light of national objectives. The vision of the NITI Aayog will then provide a framework national 'agenda' for the Prime Minister and the Chief Minister to provide impetus to."

2.1. This has simply not been done as yet, although nearly four years have since elapsed. 'The Three Year Action Agenda' published by NITI Aayog (Annexure 6) does not even mention "shared vision" anywhere; nor is there any mention of it in the PMO's letter dated 09.05.2016 containing guidelines for the preparation of "National Development Agenda" (Annexure 7).

2.2. Incidentally, the term 'agenda' is somewhat odd and obnoxious and does not properly convey the idea intended to be conveyed 'Agenda' literally means a list of things to be done or items of business to be considered at a meeting, generally a business meeting. 'Plan' is probably a more appropriate word for conveying the thought or the idea sought to be expressed.

2.3. The phrase "shared vision" has also been used in the "Approach to the Ninth Five Year Plan (1997-2002)" the relevant part of which may be quoted, as the observations made therein are of a general nature, which are valid even today:

> "The Planning Commission believes that the principal task of planning in a federal system is to evolve a shared vision of and a shared commitment to the national objective and the development strategy not only in the Government at all levels but also among all other economic agents. No development strategy can be successful unless each component of the economy works towards a common purpose with the full realisation of the role that has to be played within the overall structure of responsibilities."
>
> ".... recognising the federal nature of the Indian system, the planning process has to develop a common policy stance which would be adopted both by the Centre and the States. The role of planning would, therefore, involve considerable degree of policy coordination between the Centre and the States, and between the States and the sub-state level tiers of Government.

2.4. The observations made in the Approach Paper to the Ninth Five Year Plan quoted above are relevant in the context of evolving "a shared vision of national development priorities" by NITI Aayog, which "will then provide a framework national agenda". However, the 'Agenda' has already been prepared without first evolving a 'shared vision'. This Agenda is stated to be based on extensive discussions with, and inputs from, the central ministries and state governments. The Governing Council of the NITI Aayog, consisting of the Prime Minister as its Chairperson and several Union Ministers and State Chief Ministers as Members, extensively deliberated on the document in its draft form at its meeting on 23rd April, 2017. This final document incorporates the comments made at the meeting and those received subsequently from Chief Ministers." There is no clear indication in this 'Agenda' as to what exactly is to be done, by whom and within what time-frame; what are the monetary and other resources required and how and by whom the required resources would be made available; nor is there any indication of how and by whom the progress of implementation would be monitored and timely remedial action taken. Such an 'Agenda' is likely to remain only on paper; and the enormous amount of money spent on consultants, etc. would in that case be sheer waste.

3. The second objective of NITI Aayog is stated to be as follows:

> "To foster co-operative federalism through structured support initiatives and mechanisms with the States on a continuous basis, recognizing that strong States make a strong nation".

3.1. In Modi's model of development there is no planning body at the national level to which the states have to submit their Annual Development Plans indicating necessary details of the development schemes being implemented and the new schemes proposed to meet new challenges, the financial resources available and additional resources to be mobilised to meet the requirements, and other relevant details. Having discontinued the time tested practice of preparation of Annual Development Plans of the States, submission of those plans to the then existing Union Planning Commission, discussion and finalisation of such Plans with provisions for mobilisation of necessary funds, there is no way "to foster co-operative federalism" or strengthening the states "through structured support initiatives", which remain non-existent. In this scheme of things, it would not be possible to implement most of the points mentioned as "objectives" in para 12 of the Cabinet Resolution dated 01.01.2015. It may be only through Central Sector and Centrally Sponsored Schemes already being implemented and monitored by the concerned Central Government Ministries or other agencies that the Aayog may contribute to the development process in the States after the abolition of the Union Planning Commission.

4. India is a federation of twenty-nine states and seven Union Territories differing vastly in size and cultural and natural heritage and endowment from each other—in many cases speaking different languages and with different cultural traits, social structures, religious practices, resource endowment and consequent development

potential; in some cases different ethnic groups with different cultural traits and religious practices, different levels of socio-economic development and correspondingly different development potential. Such divers social, political and economic entities have all come under the umbrella of one Constitution which clearly defines and demarcates spheres of their respective rights, duties, powers and responsibilities, as well as common rights and duties. These states co-operate and often compete with each other in their bid to promote some cause or draw upon some common source of a natural resource (e.g., river water for irrigation or other purposes), which necessitate creation of a suitable institution to settle their claims and counter-claims in a spirit of mutual accommodation and goodwill. The social, economic or cultural relations of these states may sometimes be strained and embittered resulting in avoidable conflicts for resolving which mutually acceptable mechanism or methods have to be devised. Several such thoughts come to mind whenever we think of co-operative and competitive federalism. Inter-state Council and recently abolished National Development Council and the Union Planning Commission have also been some of the institutions which served as mediators in resolving such conflicting claims, and promoting actions and practices which minimised their occurrence and paved the way for harmony, peace and healthy and mutually beneficial competition between states or state level entities.

5. Six-and-a half decades of planning in India have been guided and governed by certain socio-economic realities of the country and constitutional imperatives: **Firstly,** the planning process had to take cognizance of the essentially federal character of the Indian polity.

Secondly, socio-economic planning being in the 'concurrent list', both the centre and the states have the constitutional authority to formulate and implement plans for socio-economic development, and have to properly coordinate their planning activities so as to ensure the formulation and effective implementation of an integrated national plan as well as the state plans, which need to be consistent with the perspectives, objectives, approaches and strategies of the national plan. In this context, sudden abolition of a national planning body like the Union Planning Commission without an open public debate, a debate in the Union Parliament and discussion on the proposal in the National Development Council and the Inter State Council has been a blatantly undemocratic and unconstitutional act detrimental to the federal structure and contrary to the federal principles on which our political and economic system is essentially based. **Thirdly**, differences in natural endowments, physiographic features and socio-economic conditions in different parts of a vast country like India have given rise to regional disparties and imbalances, which need to be removed/corrected to the extent feasible. Regional disparities also imply differences in development needs and priorities, potential and prospects which could be taken care of only if a planning exercise is done at the national level. **Fourthly**, after the abolition of the Planning Commission, the Ministry of Finance of the Central Government and the constitutional body Finance Commission have to ensure sufficient devolution of funds to the states to meet their genuine developmental needs determined on the basis of certain objective criteria and principles. **Fifthly**, there are some states with very weak resource base and very little capacity to mobilize their own resources necessitating a special dispensation to enable them to meet their genuine developmental needs. After the abolition of the Planning Commission, this responsibility too has come to the Ministry of Finance now.

6. The third objective to be achieved by NITI Aayog is to develop mechanisms to formulate credible plans at the village level and aggregate these progressively at higher levels of government.

6.1. The Constitution Seventy-Third Amendment Act, 1992 came into force on April 24, 1993 to give constitutional status to the Panchayati Raj institutions. The salient features of this Act are:

1. It provides for a 3-tier system of Panchayati Raj for all States having a population of more than 20 lakhs–Panchayats, Intermediate Panchayats and District Panchayats.
2. Panchayat elections to be held regularly every five years.
3. Reservation of seats for Scheduled Castes, Scheduled Tribes and women (not less than 33%).
4. State Finance Commission to be appointed to make recommendation regarding the financial powers of the Panchayats.
5. District Planning Committee to be constituted to prepare draft development plan for the district.

6.2. Under the Act, Gram Sabha has been vested with powers relating to:

- Ownership of Minor Forest Produce
- Development Plans Approval
- Selection of Beneficiaries under various programmes
- Consultation on land acquisition
- Management of minor water bodies
- Control of mineral leases
- Regulation/Prohibition of sale of intoxicants
- Prevention of alienation of laud and restoration of unlawfully alienated land of STs
- Managing village markets
- Control of money lending to STs
- Control of institutions and functionaries in all social sectors.

6.3. The Ministry of Rural Development extends limited financial assistance to the States in their effort to train and create awareness among the elected members of Panchayats and Panchayat functionaries.

6.4 A copy of the Guidelines for District Plans in the Eleventh Five Year Plan is at Annexure 10. A copy of the Second Round Table of State Ministers of Panchayati Raj, Mysore 28th-29th August, 2004 is also at Annexure 11.

6.5 It may be pointed out that development needs and problems at the Village Panchayat, Intermediate Panchayat, District Panchayat and higher levels may be different. *The development plans prepared at these levels cannot, therefore, be aggregated: they have to be consistent with and complimentary to each other to the extent feasible.*

7. Economic strategy and policy are to be decided by the concerned Union Ministries in consultation with experts/advisers in their respective Ministries and Secretariats. NITI Aayog can only provide some inputs. As regards interests of national security, generally the decision may need to be taken at the level of the Home Minister or the Defence Minister or the Prime Minister himself depending on the nature of the issues involved, which are generally of a classified/confidential nature to be dealt with at Secretary/ Minister level only.

8. The sections of the society which may be at the risk of not benefiting adequately from economic progress would need to be identified, e.g., small vendors, vegetable sellers, agricultural labour, powerloom and handloom weavers, carpet weavers, masons, unskilled

labour and many more such low income categories of people. The concerned Ministries and the Labour Ministry may identify and locate people in these categories and cover them with schemes for improving their skills, providing them improved tools, and working space and marketing facilities for their products to raise their income levels and earning capacities.

5

Shared Vision and Co-operative Federalism

As already mentioned in the previous chapter, according to the Cabinet Resolution dated 01 January, 2015 setting up NITI Aayog, the first objective of the Aayog is "to evolve a shared vision of national development priorities, sectors and strategies with the active involvement of states in the light of national objectives". Four years have since elapsed, but nothing of the kind has yet been done, nor is there any indication of any movement in that direction.

2. Mobilisation and assessment of resources and their sector/sub-sector and scheme/programme-wise allocation according to a mutually agreed plan are vital to the process of planned development, as well as for evolving shared vision of national and State priorities. Both the States and the erstwhile Planning Commission had been partners in this endeavour. With the Planning Commission being abolished, and its successor NITI Aayog abandoning this role, there can be no question of evolving a "shared vision" of any kind now; and any claim to do so is hollow and baseless.

3. The second objective of NITI Aayog as per the aforesaid Cabinet Resolution is "to foster co-operative federalism through structured support initiatives and mechanism with the states on a continuous basis, recognising that strong states make a strong nation."

3.1. It is pertinent to quote the observations on co-operative federalism in the 9th Five Year Plan (Vol. I), which are valid even now:

> "In a vast country like ours, the spirit of co-operative federalism should guide the relations between the centre and the states on the one hand, among different states and between the states and the Panchayati Raj Institutions (PRIs) and the Urban Local

Bodies (ULBs) on the other. The essence of co-operative federalism is that the centre and the State Governments should be guided by the broader national concerns of using the available resources for the benefit of the people. Co-operative federalism encourages the Government at different levels to take advantage of a large national market, diverse and rich natural resources and the potential of human capabilities in all parts of the country and from all sections of the society for building a prosperous nation. Co-operative federalism makes it possible to raise all the available resources by the Government at different levels in a coordinated way and channel them for use for the common good of the people. This requires a harmonious relationship and co-operative spirit between the Centre and the States and among the states themselves. While a healthy competition among the states for evolving efficient and socially desirable policies and programmes is welcome, any competition which nullifies each other's advantages in development and erodes the resource base of the states should be avoided. Co-operative federalism is intended to ensure a minimum bundle of basic services and a nationally acceptable level of living for all the people of the country."

4. In the Cabinet Resolution setting up the NITI Aayog it has not been spelt out as to what exactly is meant by "structural support initiative and mechanisms with the states on a continuous basis"; and how these would make both the states and the nation strong in the present context.

5. Three Year Action Agenda, 2017-18 to 2019-20 offering ambitious proposals for policy changes within a relatively short period makes no mention of any efforts made or proposed for involving the States and the Central Ministries to evolve any shared vision of policies and priorities. This Agenda is based on the "written inputs" received from hundreds of individuals, generally from academic institutions, and consultation with about three hundred experts in Agriculture, Trade, Industry and Services, Energy, Governance, Environment and Forests, etc. with no indication of what were their views, and how they have been made use of in the "Three Year Action Agenda."

5.1. The "Three Year Action Agenda" proposes a path to achieve all round development of India and its people as a part of Fifteen Year Vision to be outlined in a separate document, which is yet to come.

This "Agenda" differs from a 'plan' as it neither indicates the time-frame, nor the implementing agency, nor the resources required and how and by whom they would be mobilised, what part will be implemented by the Centre (the concerned Central Ministry) and what part by the concerned State (indicating the name of the State); and who would raise the resources required, how and within what time-frame, are all questions which remain unanswered. Such a "shared vision", if it is so, is of no avail, and meaningless.

5.2. Annual Plan formulation exercise every year gave an opportunity to both the senior officers of the State Govt. and the concerned Advisers of the Planning Commission, besides the Senior Ministers and Chief Ministers of the States, to interact with the concerned functionaries of the Planning Commission regarding the States' Annual Plan proposals; and subsequently remain in touch throughout the year. With the total abandoning of this role by the NITI Aayog, there is hardly any opportunity left on a regular basis for mutual consultation and interaction face to face. This has indeed been a real blow to co-operative federalism, as it has virtually choked the most important channel of continuous contact and communication between the Aayog and the State Government functionaries—thereby dealing a deadly blow to co-operative federalism. Ministry of Finance, to which this function has now been transferred, is not equipped to perform it in a manner which may promote co-operative federalism.

5.3. With the abolition of the Planning Commission, the process of Annual Plan Formulation of the States on a continuous and regular basis necessary for evolving a shared vision and promoting co-operative federalism too has vanished.

5.4. The erstwhile Planning Commission had during its sixty-five years existence formulated twelve Five Year Plans for the whole country; and Annual Plans based thereon prepared by all States and Union Territories were discussed, finalized and approved in the Annual Plan meetings held in the Planning Commission thereafter. The Planning Commission remained in constant touch with the States through their State Plan Advisers and concerned Subject Advisers to sort out any problems arising in the course of implementation. Shared vision and co-operative federalism evolved and became a reality during this entire process. There would obviously be no occasion or scope for such close continuous contacts and interaction between the NITI Aayog and the States and UTs now.

6

Elimination of Poverty

The Cabinet Resolution dated 01 January, 2015 abolishing Planning Commission and setting up NITI Aayog says: "From being preoccupied with survival, our aspirations have soared and toady we seek elimination, rather than alleviation of poverty". After this brief passing comment on poverty, there is not even a reference to or mention of poverty anywhere in this resolution. On the 16th March, 2015 NITI Aayog had issued an order setting up a "Task Force on Elimination of Poverty in India" "under the chairmanship of Vice Chairman, NITI Aayog, whose terms of reference include preparation of "a roadmap for the elimination of poverty". This Task Force had to "ensure that reports, of the Task Force of the States are available by June 15, 2015". Thereafter the Aayog will process those reports to prepare its own report within next two weeks. There is no mention of further progress in this endeavour in the Annual Report, 2015-16, 2016-17 and 2017-18 of the Aayog.

2. NITI Aayog has been given the role of coordinating 'Transforming our World: the 2030 Agenda for Sustainable Development (SDGs)' for achievement during 2016-2030 of which Goal 1 is 'End poverty in all its forms everywhere.' According to this publication, the all India Poverty Head Count Ratio (PHCR) has been brought down from 47% in 1990 to 21% in 2011-2012."

3. In the Approach to the Fifth Plan (1974-79), it is observed that during the two decades since the inception of planning there has been a sizeable increase in average per capita income and consequent improvement in living conditions everywhere, "even in the most backward districts". "Yet large numbers have remained poor". "The existence of poverty is incompatible with the vision of an advanced,

prosperous, democratic, egalitarian and just society implied in the concept of a socialist pattern of development. In fact, it holds a potential threat to the unity, integrity and independence of the country. Elimination of poverty must, therefore, have the highest priority."

4. 'Sixth Five Year Plan, 1980-85–A Framework' made several significant points relating to removal of poverty:

(i) "An increase in the productive potential of the economy is an essential condition for finding effective solutions to the problems of poverty... the hardest core of poverty is to be found in rural areas, rural artisans, scheduled castes, scheduled tribes and socially and economically backward classes."

(ii) The household will remain the basic unit of poverty eradication in target group oriented programmes. ...Hence, each household below the poverty line will have to be assisted through an appropriate package of technologies, services and asset transfer programmes."

(iii) "Even for those already employed as wage earners, the problem may be of low wages, which makes strict enforcement of minimum wages legislation all the more essential.

(iv) "The rural and urban poor also require facilities at reasonable costs in many other areas like an efficient public distribution system, public transport system to place of work and community kitchens".

(v) "An effective land reforms programme designed to redistribute surplus land among the landless and farmers with uneconomic holdings could make a significant contribution to raising the incomes and productivity of the rural poor. Consolidation of holdings for better land and water management and village planning should also be continued vigorously."

(vi) "...village communities/panchayat will have to be enabled to prepare plans through which they can optimize the returns from their resource endowments in agricultural, animal husbandry, fisheries and allied sectors."

5. The approach to the Seventh Five Year Plan, 1985-90 makes several useful observations related to poverty alleviation:

5.1. "The tendency to view poverty alleviation in isolation has to be given up, and effective linkages have to be forged with other developmental activities in the rural areas to ensure that the flow of benefits from all these schemes converge on the poverty stricken group as a package".

"The core of the anti-poverty programmes lies in the endowment of income-generating assets on those who have little or none of those. Hence, redistributive land reforms and security of tenure to the informal tenants have to be directly integrated with the anti-poverty package of programmes."

5.2. "The poverty alleviation and rural employment oriented porgrammes should ensure the kind of development that would shift a sizeable part of the rural population from agriculture to the secondary and tertiary sectors. In this context, the further development on an extensive basis, of agro-based industries is of great importance. A logical corollary of the implementation of programmes that will increase rural incomes and rural employment will be the production of consumer items in rural areas with guaranteed marketing arrangements. This would revive a number of handicrafts and hand-made items. This situation should be utilised to give considerable fillip to the handloom industry and increase its production."

5.3. There is considerable "disguised unemployment" in agriculture in India; which means that a large number of people, though visibly employed there, are just there making no positive contribution to production, i.e., their marginal productivity is zero or even negative which means their withdrawl from agriculture will not result in any perceptible decline in total agricultural production. Such surplus agricultural labourers working in their own small farms need to be identified and shifted and provided gainful employment in small agro-based or other production/manufacturing units producing, preferably, exportable small goods, which could earn valuable foreign exchange also. NGOs could play a significant role is this endeavour, by identifying and arranging shifting of such labour to nearby sites where they could be assisted in setting up small manufacturing units of preferably small exportable items to be identified. State Agriculture and Industries Department together could aid and assist this process by arranging necessary inputs like land, finance, supply of raw materials, marketing/export and training.

5.4. "Measures for the protection of Schedule Castes and Scheduled Tribes and other weaker sections from iniquitous practices leading to the alienation of their land will have to be strengthened. The strategy of Special Component Plan for development of Scheduled Castes aiming at economic and educational development and bringing about improvement in their working and living conditions launched in the Sixth Plan period has given a clear direction to the economic and social advancement of Scheduled Castes. The pace and quality of its implementation need to be considerably geared up and intensified ...."

6. The Eighth Five Year Plan acknowledges that "**the problem of poverty could not be tackled by growth**, which itself was slow over a long period of time. Hence, direct intervention through poverty alleviation programmes became necessary."

6.1. The Eight Plan further observed that "an innovative approach to development is needed which is based on a re-examination and re-orientation of the role of the government, the harnessing of the latent energies of the people through people's involvement in the process of nation building and creation of an environment which encourages and builds up people's initiative rather than their dependence on the Government, and which sets free the forces of growth and modernisation. The State has to play more of a facilitating role and has to concentrate on protecting the interests of the poor and the underprivileged".

6.2. Besides reiterating that eradication of poverty and provision of basic minimum services are vital for improving the quality of life, the Ninth Five Year Plan stressed that rapid economic growth "has strong poverty reducing effects; and "a focus on accelerated growth will also help in realising the objective of alleviating poverty."

6.3. "The poverty alleviation and rural employment oriented programme should ensure the kind of development that would shift a sizeable part of the rural population from agricultural to the secondary and tertiary sectors. In this context, further development on an extensive basis, of agro-based industries is of great importance. A logical corollary of the implementation of programmes that will increase rural incomes and rural employment will be the production of consumer items in rural areas with guaranteed marketing arrangement. This would revive a number of handicrafts and hand-made items. This situation should be utilised to give considerable fillip to the handloom industry and increase its production."

6.4. "Measures for the protection of Schedule Castes and Scheduled Tribes and other weaker sections from inequitous practices leading to the alienation of their land will have to be strengthened. The strategy of Special Component Plan for development of Scheduled Castes aiming at their economic and educational development and bringing about improvement in their working and living conditions launched in the Sixth Plan period has given a clear direction to the economic and social advancement of Scheduled Castes. The pace and quality of its implementation need to be considerably geared up and intensified ..."

6.5. The Eight Plan further observed that "an innovative approach to development which is based on a re-examination and re-orientation of the role of the government, the harnessing of the latent energies of the people through people's involvement in the process of nation building and the creation of an environment which encourages and builds up people's initiative rather than their dependence on the Government, and which sets free the forces of growth and modernisation is necessary. The state has to play more of a facilitating role and has to concentrate on protecting the interests of the poor and the underprivileged."

6.6 Besides reiterating that eradication of poverty and provision of basic minimum services are vital for improving the quality of life, the Ninth Five Year Plan stressed that rapid economic growth "has strong poverty reducing effects; and" a focus an accelerated growth will also help in realising the objective of alleviating poverty."

6.7 Estimates of Poverty in Rural and Urban Areas

7.1. The Planning Commission constituted an Expert Group under the Chairmanship a Prof. Suresh D. Tendulkar to review the methodology for estimation of poverty. The Tendulkar Committee submitted its report computing poverty lines and poverty ratios for 2004-05 in December 2009. Using the same methodology, the Committee also computed poverty lines and poverty ratios for 2004-05, which were accepted by the Planning Commission.

7.2. Subsequently, the Planning Commission made estimates of poverty for 2009-10 which were released through a Press Note on 19th March, 2012.

7.3. As several representations were received suggesting that the Tendulkar Poverty Line was too low, in June 2012 the Planning Commission constituted an Expert Group under the Chairmanship of Dr. C. Rangarajan to review the methodology for the measurement of poverty. The Planning Commission has updated the poverty estimate for the year 2011-12 according to Tendulkar Committee methodology.

Percentage and Number of Poor Estimated by Tendulkar Method Using Mixed Reference Period (MRP)

	Poverty Ratio (%)			*Number of Poor (million)*		
	Rural	*Urban*	*Total*	*Rural*	*Urban*	*Total*
1. 1993-99	50.1	31.8	45.3	328.6	74.5	403.7
2. 2004-05	41.8	25.7	37.2	326.3	80.8	407.1
3. 2011-12	25.7	13.7	21.9	216.5	52.8	269.3
Annual Average Declines: 1993-94 to 2004-05 (percentage points per annum)	0.75	0.55	0.74			
Annual Average Decline: 2004-05 to 2011-12 (percentage points per annum)	2.32	1.69	2.18			

7.4. The above table brings out the following significant facts:

1. The total Poverty Ratio declined from 45.3% in 1993-94 to 37.2% in 2004-05 and 21.9% in 2011-12.
2. The decline in Rural Poverty was much higher—50.1% in 1993-94 to 41.8% in 2004-05 and 25.7% in 2011-12, the corresponding figures for Urban Poverty being 31.8%, 25.7% and 13.7%, respectively.
3. During the eleven year period 1993-94 to 2007-05, the decline in poverty ratio was 0.74 percentage points per year, which increased to 2.18 percentage points per year over the seven year period 2004-05 to 2011-12—about three times higher.

7.5. State specific poverty lines for 2011-12, which are part of the Press Note on Poverty Estimate released by the Planning Commission in July 2013 (which is the source of the data presented above) are as shown in the following statement:

S. No.	*States*	*Monthly per capita (Rs.)*	
		Rural	*Urban*
1.	Andhra Pradesh	860	1009
2.	Arunachal Pradesh	930	1,060
3.	Assam	828	1,008
4.	Bihar	778	923
5.	Chhattisgarh	738	849
6.	Delhi	1,145	1,134
7.	Goa	1,090	1,134
8.	Gujarat	932	1,152
9.	Haryana	1,015	1,169
10.	Himachal Pradesh	913	1,064
11.	Jammu & Kashmir	891	988
12.	Jharkhand	748	974
13.	Karnataka	902	1,089
14.	Kerala	1,018	987
15.	Madhya Pradesh	771	897
16.	Maharashtra	967	1,126
17.	Manipur	1,118	1,170
18.	Meghalaya	888	1,154
19.	Mizoram	1,066	1,155
20.	Nagaland	1,270	1,302
21.	Odisha	695	861
22.	Punjab	1,054	1,155
23.	Rajasthan	905	1,002
24.	Sikkim	930	1,226
25.	Tamil Nadu	880	937
26.	Tripura	798	920
27.	Uttarakhand	880	1,082
28.	Uttar Pradesh	768	941
29.	West Bengal	783	981
30.	Puducherry	1,301	1,309
	All India	816	1,000

Note: Computed as per Tendulkar method on Mixed Reference Period (MRP).

7

Regional Planning and Special Development Programmes for Identified Backward Areas

Regional disparities or imbalances have been existing in a large country like India largely due to differences in resource endowment, geographical features, availability of infra-structural facilities and physiographic factors (e.g., existence of deserts, proneness to floods and terrain condition). Special measures may be needed for the development of such regions or areas within the states.

2. It is necessary to draw a distinction between backward or economically relatively less developed states and backward areas within a state. All Special Category States (Assam, Meghalaya, Nagaland, Manipur, Tripura, Sikkim, Jammu and Kashmir and Himachal Pradesh) which have a weak resource base and consequently relatively low capacity to mobilize financial resources, may be considered to be backward states as well. Similarly, all non-special category states, whose per capita income is below the national average (Bihar, Uttar Pradesh, Madhya Pradesh, Odisha, Rajasthan and Andhra Pradesh), can also be said to be backward states. Within these economically backward states or other states, there may be areas or pockets of backwardness. Many states have, in fact, identified certain areas within their territory as backward and have been adopting an addititive funding approach to bring about accelerated development of such areas. Some such areas are as follows:

1. Border areas in Gujarat.
2. Mewat areas comprising 6 blocks of Nuh, Ferozepur, Tharika, Nagina, Punhana and Tauru in Gurgaon district and Hatin in Faridabad districts.

3. Leh district, Kargil district, Rajouri, Poonchh and Doda districts.
4. In Kerala—Wynad, Malapuram, Idukki, Kasergoda.
5. In Meghalaya—Vidarbha and Marathwada regions.
6. In Meghalaya—Border areas.
7. In Nagaland—Tuensang and Man districts, Meluri Sub-Division is Phok district, Aghunate and Satai areas in Zunnhabote district, Peren sub-division of Kohima district and Bhandari Sub-Division in Vokha district.
8. Bundelkhand region in Uttar Pradesh.
9. In West Bengal (i) Jhargram region of Midnapur Division (ii) North Bengal and (iii) Sundarbans.

3. 'Regional Planning' implies:

(a) The existence of identifiable regions having distinct territorial limits and geographical or other characteristic features.
(b) Differences or disparities in the resource endowment and infrastructural facilities in different regions giving rise to disparities in their levels of development and the rate of growth.
(c) The need for exploiting the comparative advantages of each region and establishing inter-regional linkages for national development, and for balanced growth of all.

4. An Inter-Ministry Task Group on Growing Regional Imbalances was set up by the Planning Commission on 4th August, 2004, which gave its report in January 2005. One of the recommendations made by this Group was setting up "a Backward Districts Grant Fund" to be operated as such (rather than Backward States) to ensure that there is a focus on less developed parts within states, even those that are otherwise considered developed. The Fund should cover 115 most backward districts out of 170 districts identified as backward including 55 Extremist Affected Districts.

5. A total of 115 districts have been identified for rapid transformation on the basis of objective criteria including "education, health, nutrition, basic infrastructure like rural roads and connectivity, rural household electrification, access to potable water and individual toilets, etc. These districts include 35 districts which are affected by violence by Left Wing Extremists". "For all these 115 districts, senior level Government officers (Additional Secretary/Joint Secretary) have been appointed as Prabhari Officers" (Annexure 13).

6. Copies of Press Information Bureau, Government of India NITI Aayog's letter dated 23 November, 2017 regarding the first meeting a Prabhari Officers chaired by the Cabinet Secretary on the 24th November is at Annexure 14. A copy of another note dated 02 January, 2012 titled 'Backward Region's Grant Fund' indicating the objectives of the Fund is also at Annexure 15.

8

Panchayati Raj Institutions and District Planning

The Constitution 73rd Amendment Act, 1992 came into force on April 24, 1993 giving constitutional status to the Panchayati Raj institutions enabling them to acquire the status and dignity of viable and responsive people's bodies. This was done in pursuance of Article 40 of the Constitution which enshrines one of the Directive Principles of State Policy that the state shall take steps to organize village panchayats and endow them with such powers and authority as may be necessary to enable them to function as units of self-government. Accordingly a new part has been added to the Constitution providing for, among other things:

- Gram Sabha in a village or group of villages.
- Panchayats at village and other levels.
- Offices of Chairperson of Panchayats at such levels.
- Reservation of seats for the Scheduled Castes and Scheduled Tribes in proportion to their population for membership of Panchayats and office of Chairpersons in Panchayats at each level.
- Reservation of not less than one-third of the seats for women.
- Fixing tenure of five years for Panchayats and holding elections within six months in the event of supersession of any Panchayat.
- Disqualifications for membership of Panchayats.
- Devolution by the State Legislature of powers and responsibilities upon the Panchayats with respect to the preparation of plans for economic development and social justice and for the implementation of development schemes.

- Sound finance of the Panchayats by securing authorization from State Legislatures for grant-in-aid to the Panchayats from the Consolidated Fund of the State, as also assignment to or appropriation by the Panchayats of the revenues of designated taxes, tolls and fees.
- Setting up a Finance Commission within one year of the proposed amendment and thereafter every 5 years to review the financial position of the Panchayats.
- Auditing of accounts of the Panchayats.
- Powers of State Legislatures to make provisions with respect to election to Panchayats under the superintendence, direction and control of the Chief Electoral Officer of the States.
- Application of the provisions of the said Part to Union Territories.
- Excluding certain States and areas from the application of the provisions of the said part.
- Barring the interference by courts in electoral matters relating to Panchayats.

2. The 73rd Amendment Act, 1992 provides for a 3-tier system of Panchayati Raj in all States having a population of more than twenty lakhs. Panchayats at the village, intermediate and district levels shall be constituted in every State except in a State having a population not exceeding twenty lakhs in which Panchayats at intermediate level may not be constituted. Panchayat elections are to be held regularly every five years. The number of seats reserved for Scheduled Castes and Scheduled Tribes shall be in the same proportion as their population in the total population of the Panchayat area. Not less than one-third of the total number of seats so reserved shall be reserved for women belonging to the Scheduled Castes or Scheduled Tribes, as the case may be.

Gram Sabha

3. The "Gram Sabha" or the general assembly of villagers has a key role in the Panchayati Raj set up. Gram Sabha means a body consisting of persons registered in the electoral rolls relating to a village comprised within the area of Panchayat at the village level. In the Gram Sabha meeting, the rural poor, the women and the marginalised people now get an opportunity to join in the decision making on matters relating to

their lives. Proper functioning of this institution is necessary for the participatory democracy at the grass root level and for transparency and accountability of all Panchayati Raj institutions and processes.

- Gram Sabha should meet at least every quarter, preferably on the Republic Day, Labour Day, Independence Day and Gandhi Jayanti.
- Discuss and decide the development works that need to be taken up and their order of priority.
- Suggest measures for greater economy and efficiency in the functioning of the Panchayats.
- Discuss the Annual Budget of the Panchayat and any other important or urgent matter affecting the community living.

The Provisions of the Panchayats (Extension to the Scheduled Areas) Act, 1956.

4. This Act extends Panchayats to the tribal areas of eight States, namely, Andhra Pradesh, Bihar, Gujarat, Himachal Pradesh, Maharashtra, Madhya Pradesh, Odisha and Rajasthan. It has come into force on 24th December, 1996. Except Rajasthan and Bihar, all States have passed laws to give effect to the provisions contained in the Act.

4.1 Under the Act, Gram Sabha has been vested with powers for—

- Ownership of Minor Forest Produce
- Approval of Development Plans
- Selection of beneficiaries under various programmes
- Consultation on land acquisition
- Management of minor water bodies
- Control of mineral leases
- Regulation/prohibition of sale of intoxicants
- Prevention of alienation of land and restoration of unlawfully alienated land of Scheduled Tribes
- Management of village markets
- Control of money lending to Scheduled Tribes
- Control of institutions and functionaries in all social sectors

Training and Awareness Generation Programmes

5. Ministry of Rural Development extend limited financial assistance

to the States in their effort to train and create awareness among the elected members of Panchayats and functionaries. The State Governments are being asked to conduct such training courses. The Ministry has also been providing financial assistance through the Council for Advancement of People's Action & Rural Technology (CAPART) to the non-governmental organisations for conducting training and awareness generation programmes on Panchayati Raj. The Ministry also commissions research and evaluation studies related to Panchayati Raj from voluntary organisations/institutions.

District Planning

6. Article 243ZD of the Constitution lays down how a District Planning Committee shall be constituted in every State "to consolidate the plans prepared by the Panchayats and the Municipalities in the district and prepare a draft development plan for the district as a whole."

Ministers-in-charge of Panchayati Raj in the States met in Mysore in the "Second Round Table of State Ministers of Panchayati Raj" on 28-29th August, 2004 in "the spirit of co-operative federalism" and recommended "points of action" relating to Panchayati Raj as set out in Para IX of the Constitution and related provisions, particularly Article 243 ZD, for joint acceptance by the Centre and the States. These points are contained in the minutes of this meeting at Annexure 11. As the Union Planning Commission has been abolished w.e.f. 01.01.2015, and its successor NITI Aayog is not concerned with planning at any level—Central, State or Sub-state levels—the States could perhaps take up the matter with the Ministry of Planning and the Ministry of Rural Development informing them that they are accepting and acting in accordance with these points of action.

9
Objectives and Achievements of NITI Aayog

Objectives and Functions

The Objectives and Functions of NITI Aayog as spelt in its Annual Report, 2016-17, briefly, are as follows:

(i) To serve as a think tank of the Government of India.
(ii) To work closely with the State Governments.
(iii) Serve as a knowledge Hub.
(iv) Monitoring progress in the implementation of policies and programmes of the Government of India.
(v) Evolving a shared vision of national development with the active involvement of the States.
(vi) Informing all states about the best practices developed in one or more States or in other parts of the world for their possible adoption by them.
(vii) Designing strategic and long-term policy and programme frameworks and initiatives and monitoring their progress and efficacy regularly.
(viii) Using lessons learnt from monitoring and feedback to make innovative improvements, including necessary mid-course corrections.
(ix) Activity monitoring and evaluating the implementation of programmes and initiatives.
(x) Identification of needed resources.
(xi) Publishing policy research papers on contemporary issues.
(xii) Bring out books on best practices.
(xiii) Prepare model laws to help States reform their policies.

(xiv) Organize workshops and conferences.

(xv) Serving as a repository of research on good governance and disseminating it to stakeholders for providing directional and policy inputs.

2. It may be helpful, if the objectives are comprehensively listed in the manner indicated above and got formally approved by the Governing Body. That might further facilitate and expedite the process of setting and achieving the targets, as well as monitoring and evaluating the progress of achievements, and taking timely corrective action, when and wherever needed.

3. At present, besides NITI Aayog's Annual Reports for 2014-15, 2015-16, 2016-17 and 2017-18, we have some publicity material only to know what exactly has been achieved by the activities of NITI Aayog in these four years—we have not been able to access any material giving precise information, item-wise, about the targets set, if any, and the achievements made against them, year-wise, or during this entire four years period.

4. Press Information Bureau, Government of India has published a two-and-a half page note—"Significant Achievements of NITI Aayog over the last three years" dated 22 April, 2017, which is at Annexure 5.

5. Moving ahead of Millennium Development Goals, U.N. has evolved 17 Sustainable Development Goals for achievement during 2016-2030 (Annexure 8). The SDGs cover 17 goals and 169 related targets resolved in the U.N. Summit meet, 25-27 September, 2015 in which India was represented at the level of Hon'ble Prime Minister. The task at hand for NITI Aayog is not merely to periodically collect data on SDGs, but to achieve them "maintaining high standards of quality." These SDGs are as follows:

Goal 1: End poverty in all its forms everywhere

"The all India Poverty Head Count Ratio (PHCR) has been brought down from 47% in 1990 to 21% in 2011-2012, i.e. more than halved."

Goal 2: End hunger, achieve food security and improved nutrition and promote sustainable agriculture

"500 million small farms worldwide, mostly still rain fed, provide upto 80% of food consumed in a large part of the developing world.

Investing in small holder farmers is an important way to increase food security and nutrition for the poorest, as well as food production for the local and global markets."

"In 1990, 53% of all Indian Children were Malnourished. In 2015, malnourishment declined to 40%.

Goal 3: Ensure healthy lives and promote well-being for all at all ages.

"India's Under Five Mortality (U5MR) declined from 125 per 1000 live births in 1990 to 49 per 1000 live births in 2013."

From a Maternal Mortality Rate (MMR) of 437 per 100,000 live births in 1990-91, India came down to 167 in 2009. Delivery in institutional facilities has risen from 26% in 1992-93 to 72% in 2009.

> "India has made significant strides in reducing the prevalence of HIV and AIDS across different types of high risks categories. Adult prevalence has come down from 0.45 per cent in 2002 to 0.27 per cent in 2011."

Goal 4: Ensure inclusive and equitable quality education and promote lifelong learning opportunities for all

"India has made significant progress in universalising primary education. Enrolment and completion rates of girls in primary school have improved as are elementary completion rates. The net enrolment ratio in primary education (for both sexes) is 88% (2013-14). At the national level, male and female youth literacy rate is 94% and 92%."

Goal 5: Achieve gender equality and empower all women and girls

"India is on track to achieve gender parity at all education levels, having already achieved it at the primary level. The ratio of female literacy to male literacy for 15-24 year olds is 0.91.

As of August 2015, in India, the proportion of seats in National Parliament held by women is only 12% against the target of 50%."

Goal 6: Ensure availability and sustainable management of water and sanitation for all

"The overall proportion of households in India having access to improved water sources increased from 68% in 1992-93 to 90.6% in 2011-12."

"In 2012, 59% households in rural areas and 8% in urban areas did not have access to improved sanitation facilities. Almost 600 million people in India defecate in the open, the highest number in the world."

Goal 7: Ensure access to affordable, reliable, sustainable and modern energy for all

"Energy from renewable sources—wind, water, solar, biomass and geothermal energy—is inexhaustible and cleans. Renewable energy currently constitutes 15% of the global energy mix.

"The total installed capacity for electricity generation in India has registered a compound annual growth rate of 7% (2013-14)".

"The total installed capacity of grid interactive renewable power has been showing a growth rate of over 12% (2013-14)."

Goal 8: Promote sustained, inclusive and sustainable economic growth, full and productive employment and decent work for all

"Small and medium-sized enterprises that engage in industrial processing and manufacturing are the must critical for the early stages of industrialisation and are typically the largest job creators. They make up over 98% business worldwide and account for between 50-60% of employment."

"The unemployment rate in India is estimated to be approximately 5% at All India level (2013-14). India's labour force is set to grow by more than 8 million per year."

Goal 9: Build resilient infrastructure, promote inclusive and sustainable industrialisation and foster innovation

"Manufacturing is an important employer, accounting for around 470 million jobs worldwide in 2009 or around 16% of the world's workforce of 2.9 billion. It is estimated that there were more than half a billion jobs in manufacturing in 2013."

"India's growth rate averaged 7.25% in the last five years."

"India's CO_2 emissions per capita are 1.67 (metric tons), one of the lowest in the world, the global average being around 4-5 (metric tons). In 2010, per capita annual electricity consumption was 626 kwH compared to the global average of 2977 kwH."

Goal 10: Reduce inequality within and among countries

"The Gini Coefficient of income inequality for India has risen from 33.4% in 2004 to 33.6% in 2011."

Goal 11: Make cities and human settlement inclusive, safe, resilient and sustainable

"By 2030, India is expected to be home to 6 mega-cities with populations above 10 million. Currently, 17% of India's urban population lives in slums."

Goal 12: Ensure sustainable consumption and production patterns

"India is the fourth largest GHG emitter, responsible for 5.3% of global emissions. India has committed to reduce the emission intensity of its GDP by 20 to 25% by 2020."

Goal 13: Take urgent action to combat climate change and its impacts

"India has committed to reduce the emission intensity of its GDP by 20 to 25% by 2020."

Goal 14: "Conserve and sustainably use the oceans, seas and marine resources for sustainable development

"There are some 120 species of marine mammal to be found in the world, and a fourth of these may be found in India and adjacent countries. More than 1 million people in 3561 villages of India situated along the coast are employed in marine capture fisheries."

Goal 15: Protect, restore and promote sustainable use of terrestrial ecosystems, sustainably manage forests, combat desertification, halt and reverse land degradation and halt biodiversity loss

"Forest cover in India has increased to 21.23% — an increase of 5871 sq. km, and protected areas cover to about 4.8% of the country's total land area."

"India is among the early movers on the Nagoya protocol and is committed to the Aichi targets on conserving biodiversity."

"India has 8% of the world's biodiversity with many species that are not found anywhere else in the world."

Goal 16: Promote peaceful and inclusive societies for sustainable development, provide access to justice for all and build effective, accountable and inclusive institutions at all levels

"In India, more than 20% of all pupils and one-third of all Scheduled Tribe students drop out before finishing primary education."

Goal 17: Strengthen the means of implementation and revitalize the global partnership of sustainable development

"India has the second highest number of Internet users in the world. However, the Internet penetration in the country is under 20%."

Some of the NITI Aayog's Achievements in the First Three Years as Publicised by it

1. Measuring Performance and Ranking States on Outcomes in Critical Sector

"NITI finalised indices to measure incremental annual outcomes in critical social sectors like health, education and water with a view to nudge the states into competing with each other for better outcomes, sharing best practices and innovations. District hospital index was developed to assess the performance of district hospital and monitor hospital performance with focus on outputs and outcomes. A guidebook was released on World Health Day, 2016. The Implementation phase is presently underway in collaboration with Ministry of Health and Family Welfare. Indian Statistical Institute is assisting in data analytics. NITI has also developed a Digital Transformation Index (DT), which will measure States' progress in ushering in digital economy, digital infrastructure, and digitally available government services."

Necessary planned and time-bound action to achieve these seventeen Millennium Development Goals needs to be taken by the concerned Ministries of the Government of India involving all the State Governments. NITI Aayog can play a coordinating and monitoring role. It is not yet clear how there goals are planned to be achieved by NITI, and how and within what time-frame.

2. *Sustainable Action for Transforming Human Capital (SATH)*

"SATH aimed at initiating transformation in two key social sectors, viz., education and health by hand holding states to improve their social sector indicators and providing technical support to states over three years. The states were selected based on a certain set of challenges. Uttar Pradesh, Assam and Karnataka were selected for improvement in their healthcare delivery and key health indicators. Madhya Pradesh, Odisha and Jharkhand were selected for improvement in the education sector."

3. *Ek Bharat Shrestha Bharat (EBSB)*

NITI Aayog "conceptualised EBSB to unite the country and promote excellence in all walks of life through long-term inter-state engagements in cultural exchanges and education. MOUs were entered with six paired States/UTs. Department of Higher Education, Ministry of Human Resources Development took forward the initiative. Towards further integration, 100 commonly used conversational sentences throughout India were identified and translated into 22 Indian languages, compiled as a book and widely distributed."

4. *Development Support Services to States (DSSS) for Development of Infrastructure*

"To establish a Centre-State Partnership model and reignite and establish Private Public Partnership across infrastructure sectors DSSS was launched to derisk projects and address key structural issues in project development and build institutional and organisational capacities. Out of over 450 projects received from 20 states, 11 projects from 8 states in 10 sectors were shortlisted through the challenges method, for structuring and implementation."

5. *Regulatory Reforms*

"NITI finalised the consolidation of laws for Rajasthan and the work for Jammu & Kashmir and Maharashtra is in progress."

6. *Public-Private Partnership in Health*

"Developed a guiding framework for states for the implementation of district hospital level-focus in tier II/tier III cities by engaging services of private/voluntary sector providers for achieving health goals of the government in areas of prevention, diagnosis and treatment of select Non-Communicable diseases, viz. Cardiac Sciences, Oncology and Pulmonary Sciences."

7. Resolution of Pending Issues of States with Central Ministries

"Sought pending issues with the Central Ministries from all states and UTs for expeditious resolution. Issues received from the States of Rajasthan, Himachal Pradesh, Bihar, Odisha and Puducherry have since been resolved."

8. State Human Development Report

"The States of Maharashtra, Assam, Tamil Nadu, Gujarat, Karnataka, Nagaland, Bundelkhand region and Delhi were supported for preparation of State Human Development Report."

9. Transformation of 115 Aspirational Districts

"A special initiative focusing on 115 aspirational districts which need to improve on key indicator like health, nutrition, education, basic infrastructure and poverty has been launched. The focus will be an technology and sharing of best practices. At least one aspirational district has been selected from every State and Prabhari Officers (Coordinating Officers) appointed for all the 115 districts to converge and integrate Central and State Government programmes. District Magistrate has been made the fulcrum on which the programme rests. The project would be implemented in the true spirit of co-operative federalism."

10. Promoting inclusive growth—Giving fillip to Government's Goal of Sabka Sath Sabka Vikas

"Based on recommendations made by NITI on the committed liabilities under PMS for SCs, Department of Social Justice has initiated the process for revamping the scheme to provide transparency regarding institutes, courses, etc. and also for clearing pending Central arrears.

After discontinuation of Planning and merges of Plan and Non-Plan Expenditure, new guidelines for earmarking of funds for SCs and STs in the new budgeting system have been prepared.

A report prepared on Revamping of Tribal Research Institutes (TRIs) to promote them as Top Class Research Institutes and circulated to States/UT and Ministry of Tribal Affairs for consultations.

Monitoring Framework for SCSP and TSP has been developed and circulated to the nodal Ministries for online monitoring of SCSP & TSP.

Gaps in National Policy for persons with Disabilities, 2006 have been identified and forwarded to D/o Empowerment of persons with Disabilities for revision of the policy.

Critical issues have been identified and forwarded to D/o Empowerment of persons with Disabilities for resolution towards meeting the goals of Accessible India Campaign.

A concept paper on the "Means of Livelihood in LWE Areas: Prospects of Aroma, Honey, Dairying and other traditional industries" has been circulated to the concerned Central Ministries, States and other stakeholders for their views.

Common guidelines for Implementation of CSS/CS schemes through NGOs have been prepared and circulated.

The new NGO-Darpan Portal which when live w.e.f. 06.04.2017 was developed giving electronic dynamic database of NGOs in the country. It facilitates NGOs to sign up and obtain unique ID to be eligible to apply for grants from any Central Ministry/Department."

10. Finalising the Three Year Action Agenda

"As the Government moves away from Five Year Plans and Annual Plans to long-term vision, a three-year Action Agenda covering the period from 2017-18 to 2019-20 was prepared. The action Agenda framework allows better alignment of the development strategy with the changed reality of India. The Agenda was prepared after detailed consultation with the State Governments, Union Territories, Ministries of the Central Government and the stakeholders like scientists, economists, journalists, voluntary organisation, industry associations and experts in education, health, culture, defence, transport and other fields. The action agenda covers areas ranging from agriculture, industry, services, health, education, and management of water resources, revenue and expenditure framework. It contains ambitious yet achievable proposals to achieve far reaching changes in India's economy."

11. Reform of Central Public Sector Enterprises

"After being mandated to identify CPSEs for strategic disinvestment, NITI Aayog in consultation with administrative ministries made recommendation in four trenches for strategic disinvestment in PSUs. So far, based on NITI Aayog's recommendations, more than 30 CPSEs have been approved by the Cabinet Committee on Economic Affairs for in-principle strategic disinvestment. The process of disinvestment is being carried out by DIPAM and the initial transactions are expected in the current financial year after a long gap of 14 years. In line with the Government's philosophy that government should not be in the business of business, more CPSEs are being examined for strategic disinvestment. A report was submitted to the Government on 74 sick/ loss-making/non-performing CPSEs. The recommendations are under implementation and so far more than 15 CPSEs are undergoing closure."

10

An Empirical Analysis of Certain Aspects of Planned Development in India in the Last Four Decades

An analysis of the available statistical data relating to the last few Five Year Plan periods in India brings out some significant facts.

1. Plan Outlays and Expenditure

Figures in Table 1 below reveal the following significant facts:

(i) Plan outlay as percentage of total Government expenditure was relatively very high during the Fifth Plan (1974-79), being 38.84 per cent of Total Govt. Expenditure of the Central and State Governments. This percentage increased to a record 44% during the Sixth Plan (1980-85)

In the Seventh Plan (1985-90), this percentage was 37.22 which peaked to 39.76 during the Eleventh Plan (2007-2012).

Table 1: Plan Outlays and Expenditure (Rs. Crores)

Plan Period	*Plan Outlay (Actual)*	*Total Expenditure of Central and State Govt.*	*Plan Outlay as % of Total Govt. Expenditure*
1. Fifth Plan (1974-79)	39426	101506	38.84
2. Sixth Plan (1980-85)	110467	248377	44.00
3. Seventh Plan (1965-90)	218730	594884	37.22
4. Eighth Plan (1992-97)	485457	1278631	33.95
5. Ninth Plan (1997-2002)	813998	2474127	34.73
6. Tenth Plan (2002-2007)	1255784	4236763	29.64
7. Eleventh Plan (2007-2012)	3582768	9010585	39.76

Source: Indian Public Finance Statistics, Govt. of India, Ministry of Finance, Deptt. of Economic Affairs Economic Division—Various issues.

Table 2: Outlays (Actuals) of Central States and UTs Plans (Rs. Crores)

	Central Plans	State Plans	UTs Plans	Total	As Percentage of Total		
					Central	States	UTs
1. Sixth Plan (1980-85)	57825.2	49458.2	2008.3	109291.7	52.9	45.3	1.8
2. Seventh Plan(1985-90)	127519.6	87492.4	3717.7	218729.6	58.3	40.0	1.7
3. Annual Plan (1990-91)	34254.7	23116.9	997.7	58369.3	58.7	39.6	1.7
4. Annual Plan (1991-92)	37846.5	25739.3	1165.4	64751.2	58.4	39.8	1.8
5. Eighth Plan (1992-97)	28830.0	187937.5	8589.7	48457.2	59.5	38.7	1.8
6. Ninth Plan (1997-2002)	489361.0	369839.0	Na	859200	56.95	43.04	–
7. Tenth Plan (2002-07)	893183	632456	Na	1525639	58.54	41.45	–

Source: Economic Survey, 2012-13 Statistical Appendix A-40 to A-44.

As Table 2 above would reveal, the Central Plan Outlays (Actuals) had been in the range of 52.9 per cent to 59.5 per cent of the total plan outlays of Central, states and UTs over the Sixth to Tenth Plan periods, the corresponding figures for the State Plan Outlays being 38.7 per cent in the Eighth Plan and 45.3% is the Sixth Plan period.

Table 3: Total Annual Plan Outlays (Actuals) and Total Expenditure of States (Rs. Crores)

Year	Annual Plan Outlay	Total Expenditure	Plan Outlay as % of Total Expenditure
1990-91	23116.9	80232.03	28.81
1995-96	42044.3	16676.13	25.68
2000-01	72428.6	30244.70	23.97
2005-06	142519	514572.97	27.69
2006-07	185570	610753	30.38

Source: Economic Survey, 2012-13, Govt. of India, Ministry of Finance.

The above table shows that Annual Plan Outlay of the States as % of their Total Expenditure varied in the range of 23.97 in 2000-01 to 30.38 is 2006-07.

The Table 4 shows that Annual Plan Outlays (Actuals) of the Centre had been declining. The Annual Plan Outlay as percentage of Total Expenditure of the Centre declined from 32.63% in 1990-91 to 21.80% in 2006-07.

Table 4: Total Annual Plan Outlays (Actuals) of the Centre and Total Expenditure of the Centre (Rs. Crores)

Year	*Annual Plan Outlay*	*Total Expenditure*	*Plan Outlay as % of Total Expenditure*
1990-91	34254.7	04973	32.63
1995-96	63493.7	185233	34.27
2000-01	109119.3	328265	33.24
2005-06	104638	501083	20.88
2006-07	124342	570185	21.80

Source: Economic Survey, 2012-13, Govt. of India, Ministry of Finance.

Table 5: Pattern of Plan Outlays (Actuals) Seventh to Twelfth Plan (Rs. Crores)

Head of Development	*Seventh Plan 1985-90*	*Eighth Plan 1992-97*	*Nineth Plan*	*Tenth Plan*	*Eleventh Plan 2007-12*	*Twelfth Plan 2012-17*
1	2	3	4	5	6	7
I. Agriculture & allied activities	12792.6 (5.8)	22467.2 (5.2)	42462.0 (4.9)	58933 (3.9)	136381 (3.7)	363273 (4.7)
II. Rural Development	15246.5 (7.0)	34425.4 (7.9)	74636.0 (8.7)	12198 (8.0)	301069 (8.3)	457464 (6.0)
III. Special area programme	3470.3 (1.6)	6750.1 (1.6)	3649.0 (0.4)	20879 (1.4)	26329 (0.7)	80370 (1.0)
IV. Irrigation & food control	16589.9 (7.6)	32525.3 (7.5)	55420.0 (6.5)	103315 (6.8)	210326 (5.8)	422012 (5)
V. Energy of which Power	61689.3 (28.2)	115561.1 (26.6)	222.375.0 (25.9)	403927 (26.5)	854123 (23.4)	1438466 (18.8)
	37895.3 (17.3)	79588.7 (18.3)	a	a	–	–
VI. Industry & Universals of which village small scale industries	29220.3 (13.4)	42921.7 (10.8)	65148.0 (7.6)	58939 (3.9)	153600 (4.2)	377302 (4.9)
	3249.3 (1.5)	6334.2 (1.5)	a	a	–	–
VII. Transport of which Railways	29548.1 (13.5)	55925.6 (12.9)	119373.0 (13.9)	225977 (14.8)	572443 (15.7)	1204172 (15.7)
	16549.2 (7.6)	27202.0 (6.3)	a	a	–	–
VIII. Communications	8425.5 (3.9)	25110.0 (5.8)	47280.0 (5.5)	98968 (6.5)	95380 (2.6)	80984 (1.1)
IX. Science technology & environment	30239 (1.4)	9041.7 (2.1)	18458.0 (2.1)	30424 (2.0)	87933 (2.4)	167350 (2.2)
X. General economic services	2249.6 (1.0)	4549.5 (1.0)	14580.0 (1.7)	38630 (2.5)	62523 (1.7)	305612 (4.0)
XI. Social services of which Education Medical & Public health housing	34959.7 (16.0)	79011.9 (18.2)	183273.0 (21.3)	347391 (22.8)	1102327 (0.2)	2664843 (34.7)
	7685.5 (3.5)	19599.7 (4.5)	a	a	–	–
	3688.6 (1.7)	7575.9 (1.7)	a	a	–	–
	2722.8 (1.2)	573.0 (1.2)	a	a	–	–
XII. General services	1513.8 (0.7)	1810.5 (0.4)	12496.0 (1.5)	16328 (1.1)	42283 (1.2)	107959 (1.4)
XIII. Total (I to XII)	218729.6 (100.0)	434100.0 (100.0)	859200.0 (100.0)	1525639 (100.0)	3644718 (100.0)	7669807 (100.0)
a. Central Plan	127519.6 (58.3)	434100.0 (100.0)	859200.0 (100.0)	1525639 (100.0)	3644718 (100.0)	766987 (100.0)
b. State Plans	87492.4 (40.0)	179985.0 (41.5)	369839.0 (43.0)	632456 (41.5)	–	–
c. Union Territory Plans	3717.7 (1.7)	6250.0 (1.4)	NA	NA	–	–

Source: Economic Survey, 2012-13—A-41, A-42, A-43, A-44, A-45 and A-46.

2. Pattern of Plan Outlays

Table 5 brings out of the following significant facts about the pattern of Plan Outlays:

(i) Central Plan Outlays had accounted for 57.0 to 58.5 per cent of the Total Plan Outlays over the Seventh (1985-90) to Tenth (2002-07) Plan periods.

(ii) State Plan Outlays had been in the range of the 40.0 to 43.0 per cent of total plan outlays over the Seventh to the Tenth Plan period (1985-90 to 2002-07).

(iii) Total Plan Outlays on Agriculture and Allied Activities had been declining over this entire period —5.8% of the total five year plan outlay of the Seventh Plan period (1985-90) to 5.2% of the Eighth Plan Outlay (1992-97), 4.9% of the Ninth Plan (1997-2002) and 3.9% of the Tenth Plan Outlay (2002-07).

(iv) Total Plan Outlays for Rural Development have varied from 7.0% of total plan outlays during 1985-90 to 8.7% during 1997-2002. They were 8.0% during Tenth Plan Period (2002-07).

(v) Energy claimed 28.2% of total Seventh Plan Outlay (1985-90) the corresponding figures in Eighth (1992-97), Ninth (1997-2002) and Tenth (2002-07) Plan being 26.6% , 25.9% and 26.5 % respectively.

(vi) Village and Small Scale Industries—the most labour intensive sector —accounted for mere 1.5% of total Plan Outlays during the Seventh and Eights Plan period for which figures are available. The position regarding Medical & Public Health during these two periods was almost the same —1.7% during both these plan periods.

Table 6: Plan Outlays and Developmental Expenditure of Centre and the States

Year	Plan Outlay	Development Expenditure	Total Expenditure	Plan Outlay as Percentage	
				Developmental Expenditure	Total Expenditure
1985-86	33060	38442.12	76415.35	85.99	43.26
1990-91	61518	74000.28	155141.47	83.13	39.65
1995-96	107380	126518.42	293103.50	84.87	36.63
2000-01	185737	236096.06	552124.48	78.67	33.64
2005-06	277177	418060.65	933641.76	59.12	26.47
2006-07	309912	519109.75	1086592.18	59.70	28.52
2007-08	371569	621331.81	1243597.56	59.80	29.87
2008-09	477236	770608.94	1519081.18	61.92	31.41
2009-10	529024	887629.98	1814610.4	59.59	32.62

Sources: Indian Economic Statistics-Public Finance, 1990; Indian Public Finance Statistics, 2002-2003; Indian Public Finance Statistics, 2011-2012.

3. Plan Outlays and Developmental Expenditure

Table 6 above brings out the following significant facts:

(i) Plan outlays had been continuously increasing over the period 1985-86 to 2009-10, but the development expenditure had been increasing faster during this entire period. Plan outlays as percentage of Development Expenditure had therefore been falling continuously—declining from 85.99% of Development Expenditure in 1985-86 to 59.59% in 2009-10. Similarly, Plan Outlay as percentage of Total Expenditure declined from 43.26% in 1985-86 to 32.62% in 2009-10. This continuously declining share of Plan Outlays in the Development Expenditure and Total expenditure indicated more and more development activity taking place outside the plan, which had been a welcome development.

4. Financial Resources for Annual Plans of States

Figures in Table 7 bring out the following significant facts:

(1) There has been an increase in Approved Outlays for the Annual Plans of the States by more than four times (from Rs. 30032 crores to Rs. 132958 crores) over the fourteen year period 1992-93 to 2005-06.

(2) While the Contribution of Public Sector Enterprises remained negative in all these years, except 1995-96 and 1997-98, when they were mildly positive, Balance from Current Revenues became negative in 1997-98, and did not recover thereafter being continuously negative till 2005-06. During the fourteen years 1992-93 to 2005-06, the Annual Plans of the States have been financed by 'Loans and All Other Domestic Sources', 'Central Assistance and Plans Grants by the Finance Commission under Article 275(1) of the Constitution', Central Assistance accounting for the largest share followed by loans and all other domestic sources.

5. Government Expenditure, Plan Expenditure and GDP

Table 8 brings out the following significant facts:

(1) Central Plan Expenditure had been 5.84 per cent of the GDP at market prices in 1990-91. It remained marginally above 5% (5.17%) in 1995-96 and 2000-01 (5.03%). It was below 5% in the subsequent three years and declined to below 3% in 2005-06 and 2006-07.

Table 7: Estimate of Financial Resources for the Annual Plans of States (Rs. Crores)

Year	*Domestic Resources*						
	Approved Outlay/ Expen-diture	*Balance from current revenue (inclu-ding ARM)*	*Contribu-tion of public sector enter-prises*	*Total (including loans and all other domestic sources)*	*Central Assis-tance*	*Plan Grants under Act. 275(1) (Finance Commi-ssion)*	*Total (6 + 7)*
1	2	3	4	5	6	7	
1992-93	30032	1606	–1452	13241	13369	1780	15149 (50.44)
1993-94	33695	4229	–2019	15797	14417	2231	16648 (49.40)
1994-95	38911	3474	–1010	18777	17468	2666	20134 (51.74)
1995-96	46233	1642	884	231919	20984	2058	23042 (49.84)
1996-97	54287	2349	–297	28742	23678	1867	25545 (97.05)
1997-98	46667	–4238	1009	18765	25884	2018	27902 (59.78)
1998-99	72088	–26789	–4647	41319	28527	2242	30769 (42.60)
1999-2000	78435	–26789	–2648	43449	31918	3068	34986 (44.60)
2000-01	83145	–23632	–3927	43988	35743	3414	39157 (47.09)
2001-02	83991	–0288	–4654	41050	39482	3459	42941 (51.12)
2002-03	87362	–35119	–2864	38727	45361	3274	48635 (55.67)
2003-04	89878	–28350	–3350	41145	47458	1275	48733 (57.16)
2004-05	11455	–23328	–1246	53314	56240	1901	58141 (52.16)
2005-06	132958	–14737	–1375	72296	31279	380	31659 (23.81)

Source: India Public Finance Statistics, 2011-2012, Government of India Ministry of Finance, Deptt. of Economic Affairs, Economic Division.

(2) State Plans Expenditure was 3.94% of GDP in 1990-91 and remained below 3.5% in 1995-96, 2000-01 and the four following years. In 2006-07, it recorded an increase to 4.32% of GDP at Market Prices.

(3) Developmental Expenditure of the Centre and the States combined was 12.62% of the GDP at Market Prices in 1990-91. It fell to 10.31% in 1995-96 and remained well above 10.75% in

Table 8: Government Expenditure, Plan Expenditure and GDP (₹ Crores)

Year	*Total Government Expenditure*				*Plan Expenditure*			
	Combined Centre and States		*States*		*Central Plan*	*State Plans*	*Total (including U.T. Plans)*	*GDP At Market Prices*
	Develop-mental	*Total*	*Develop-mental*	*Total*				
1	2	3	4	5	6	7	8	9
1990-91	74000.258 (12.62)	155141.47 (26.46)	49546.09 (8.45)	80232.03 (13.68)	34254.7 (5.84)	23116.9 (3.94)	58369.3 (9.95)	5862.12
1995-96	126518.42 (10.31)	293103.50 (23.89)	94440.72 (7.69)	1636.76.13 (13.34)	63493.7 (5.17)	42044.3 (3.42)	107380.4 (8.75)	122672.5
2000.01	236096.06 (10.88)	552124.48 (25.45)	168401.2 (7.76)	302149.70 (13.93)	109119.3 (5.03)	724286 (3.33)	185736.8 (8.56)	2168652
2001-02	233578.03 (0.79)	613590.99 (26.12)	179710.11 (7.65)	335586.49 (14.29)	104403.8 (4.44)	768387 (3.27)	186315.2 (7.93)	2348331
2002-03	271957.79 (10.74)	66166393 (26.14)	184286.26 (7.28)	355029.89 (14.02)	126247 (4.98)	78430 (3.09)	2102.03 (8.30)	2530663
2003-04	328666.09 (11.58)	762764.73 (26.87)	229124.41 (8.07)	422125.48 (14.87)	1322.62 (4.66)	86756 (3.05)	224827 (7.92)	2837900
2004-05	342791.42 (10.57)	824479.76 (25.42)	239478.95 (7.38)	455415.37 (14.04)	150818 (4.65)	107206 (3.30)	263665 (8.13)	3242209
2005-06	418060.65 (11.31)	933641.76 (25.27)	287002.81 (7.77)	514572.97 (13.93)	109658 (2.83)	142519 (3.85)	247177 (6.69)	3693369
2006-07	519109.75 (12.08)	1086592.18 (25.30)	355067.07 (8.26)	610753.44 (14.22)	124342 (2.89)	185570 (4.32)	309912 (7.21)	4294706

Source: Indian Pubic Finance Statistics, 2002-203, 2008-2009 and 2011-2012, Govt. of India, Ministry of Finance, Deptt. Of Economic Affairs, Economic Division Economic Survey 2011-2012 and 2012-2013 Govt. of India, Ministry of Finance, Deptt. Of Economic Affairs, Economic Division.

N.B. Figures within brackets are percentages of GDP at Market Prices.

2000-01 (10.88%) and 2001-02 (10.79%). In 2006-07, it was 12.08% of the GDP at Market Prices (Table 8).

(4) State's Developmental Expenditure as percentage of GDP at Market Prices has been varying in the range of 7.28 to 8.26 of the GDP at Market Prices over the period 1990-91 to 2006-07 (Table 8).

6. Financial Resources for Annual Plans of States

Table 9: Financial Resources for Annual Plans of States (₹ crores)

Year	Approved Outlay/ Expenditure	Balance from current (resource including ARM)	Contribution of Public Sector Enterprises	Market Loans	Term Loans from financial institutions/ corporations	Small Savings	Miscellaneous Capital Receipts	Total Domestic Resource	Central Assistance	Play Grants under Article 275 (i) (Finance Commission
1	2	3	4	5	6	7	8	9	10	11
1991-92	28063	1510 (5.38)	–1128	4200 (14.96)	1498 (5.33)	6325 (22.53)	–633	12399 (44.18)	11835 (42.17)	1333 (4.75)
1995-96	46233	1642 (3.55)	884 (1.91)	5931 (12.82)	3123 (6.75)	8344 (18.04)	–4565	3191 (0.16)	20984 (45.38)	2058 (4.45)
2000-01	83145	–3632	–3927	10727 (12.90)	14791 (17.78)	26842 (32.28)	–10624	43988 (52.90)	35743 (42.98)	3414 (4.10)
2001-02	83991	–30288	–4654	11557 (13.75)	16157 (19.23)	31960 (38.05)	–10399	41050 (48.87)	39482 (47.00)	3459 (4.11)
2002-03	87362	–35119	–2864	13635 (15.60)	14612 (16.72)	39601 (45.32)	–16285	38727 (44.32)	45361 (51.92)	3274 (3.74)
2003-04	89878	–28350	–3350	13467 (14.98)	17414 (19.37)	39232 (43.65)	–19486	41145 (45.77)	47458 (52.80)	1275 (1.41)
2004-05	111455	–3328	–1246	13641 (12.23)	15473 (13.88)	46428 (41.65)	–21974	53314 (47.83)	56240 (50.45)	1901 (1.70)
2005-06	132958	–14737	–1375	16112 (12.11)	20745 (15.60)	57878 (43.53)	–26058	72296 (54.37)	31279 (23.52)	380 (0.28)

Source: Indian Public Finance Statistics, 2011-2012, Govt. of India, Ministry of Finance, Deptt. of Economic Affairs, Economic Division.

N.B. Figures within brackets are percentage of Approved Outlay/ Expenditure.

Table 9 above provides data relating to several other constituents of State Plan resources in Columns 3, 5, 6, 7, 8 and 9 not available in Table 7. Balance from Current Revenues, including Additional Resource Mobilisation (ARM), which had been positive in 1991-92 and 1995-6 (although accounting for only 5.38% and 3.55% of Approved Outlay in these two years), began declining steeply thereafter till 2005-06, the year upto which the data have been available.

Contribution of Public Sector Enterprises has all along been negative, except in 1995-96 when it was mildly positive. Miscellaneous Capital Receipts (MCR) have shown the same persistently negative trend in these years. Only term loans from financial institutions, small savings and Market Loans have been positive over these years. Plan

Grants under Article 275(1) of the Constitution by the Finance Commission have provided a maximum of 4.75% (Rs. 1333 crores in 1991-92) and a minimum of 0.28% of Approved outlays in 2005-06. The only large and steady source of financing of Approved Annual Plan Outlays of States has been Central Assistance, providing 42 to nearly 53% of State Plan Expenditure during this period 1991-92 to 2005-06.

Table 10: Central Plan Assistance to States and their Total Revenue (₹ Crores)

Year	*Central Assistance*	*Total Revenue*	*Central Assistance as Percentage of Total Revenue*
1991-92	11835	77165.31	15.33
1995-96	20984	131654.08	15.93
2000-01	35743	219737.05	16.26
2001-02	39482	2246288.78	16.03
2002-03	45361	259774.58	17.46
2003-04	47458	304630.56	15.57
2004-05	56240	354671.47	15.85
2005-06	31279	428515.96	7.29

Source: Indian Public Finance Statistics, Govt. of India, Ministry of Finance, Deptt. of Economic Affairs, Economic Division—Various issues.

Central Plan Assistance as percentage of Total Revenue of the State was 15.33 per cent in 1991-92. This percentage kept on rising till 2002-03 when it became 17.46. Thereafter it has been declining, the rate of decline being very steep in 2005-06 at the record low of 7.29 per cent of the Total Revenue of the State.

7. Financial Performance of States and Union Territories

Figures in Table 11 below show that Haryana, Madhya Pradesh, Rajasthan, Tamil Nadu and Himachal Pradesh utilised more than hundred per cent of Tenth Plan Approved Outlay (2002-07). Similarly, Gujarat, Karnataka, Maharashtra, Uttar Pradesh and Arunachal Pradesh utilised more than 95% of the approved Tenth Plan Outlay during this period.

Actual Expenditure as percentage of Total Approved Annual Plan Outlay was more than 100% in 2009-10 in Tamil Nadu, Tripura, Delhi and Himachal Pradesh. In the preceding year 2007-08, the utilisation of Approved Annual Plan Outlay was more than 100 per cent in Haryana (108.50), Madhya Pradesh (100.29), Odisha (108.12), Rajasthan (18.52) and Tamil Nadu (101.60).

Table 11: Financial Performance of States and Union Territories (₹ crores)

	1997-98			Tenth Plan 2002-07			2007-09			2009-10		
	Originally Approved Outlay	*Actual Expendi-ture*	*Actual as % Approved*	*Originally Approved Outlay*	*Actual Expenditure*	*Actual as % Approved*	*Approved Outlay*	*Actual Expenditure*	*Actual as % Approved*	*Approved Outlay*	*Actual Outlay*	*Actual as % Approved*
1. Andhra Pradesh	3580	3707	103.54	69512	62177	89.44	30500	27171	89.08	33497	29391	87.71
2. Assam	1510	1283	84.96	12503	9302	74.39	3800	2669	70.23	6000	5023	83.71
3. Bihar	2268	1711	75.44	23864	21045	88.18	10200	9652	94.62	16000	14184	88.65
4. Gujarat	4510	3905	86.38	47482	45976	96.82	16000	15651	97.81	23500	22634	96.31
5. Haryana	1576	1304	82.74	12708	12980	102.14	5300	571	108.50	10000	9624	96.24
6. J. & K.	1552	1496	96.39	16321	14217	87.10	4850	4403	90.78	5500	5279	95.98
7. Manipur	410	345	84.14	4073	2712	66.58	1334	1337	97.30	2000	1784	89.20
8. Karnataka	4154	4424	106.99	60275	59659	98.97	17783	17227	96.87	29500	23967	81.24
9. Kerala	2851	2868	100.59	24887	19543	78.52	6950	5085	73.16	8920	774	87.15
10. Madhya Pradesh	3718	3344	89.94	33725	34003	100.82	12011	12047	100.29	16174	14610	90.33
11. Maharashtra	8393	7938	94.57	58888	56100	95.26	20200	19422	96.14	35959	27731	77.11
12. Odisha	2529	2037	80.54	15300	14099	92.15	5105	5520	108.12	9500	7728	81.34
13. Punjab	2100	2009	95.66	16645	14885	89.42	5111	5024	98.29	8600	4974	57.83
14. Rajasthan	3514	3978	113.20	33067	33735	102.02	11639	13795	118.52	17322	18023	104.04
15. Tamil Nadu	4005	4011	100.14	42351	42676	100.76	14000	14224	101.60	17500	17834	101.90
16. Uttar Pradesh	7247	5652	77.96	57140	54797	95.89	25000	24297	97.18	39000	37212	95.41
17. Tripura	440	413	93.86	3729	3383	90.72	1220	1067	87.45	1680	1736	103.33
18. West Bengal	3908	2840	72.67	29721	22396	75.35	9150	8858	96.80	14150	12122	85.66
19. Delhi	2073	1978	95.41	25026	22646	90.48	9000	8747	97.158	10000	11048	110.48
20. Meghalaya	382	249	65.18	3516	2924	83.16	1120	984	87.85	2100	1418	67.52
21. Mizoram	290	295	101.72	2970	2917	98.21	850	767	90.23	1250	1067	85.36
22. Arunachal Pradesh	600	489	81.50	4150	3460	53.37	1320	1083	82.04	2100	2016	96.00
23. Himachal Pradesh	1008	1294	128.37	7975	8526	106.90	2100	2099	99.95	2700	2808	104.00

Source: Indian Public Finance Statistics, 2011-2012, Govt. of India, Ministry of Finance, Deptt. of Economic Affairs, Economic Division.

11

Planning Commission to NITI Aayog

Response to a RTI Query

When India got independence in 1947, it was a relatively poor and less development country lacking the basic infrastructure required for rapid economic development. At that stage, the country had been caught in what Ragner Nurkse described as a "vicious circle of poverty": low income, low savings, low investment resulting in low income again. This circle had to be broken and the process reversed by increasing investment, particularly in basic infrastructure, requiring large, lumpy investments financed substantially by external aid and financial assistance from international lending institutions till the country reached the "take off" stage, when it could mobilize the required resources and technological support itself to accelerate the process of economic development. It was at this initial stage of the country's development that the Planning Commission was set up by a Government of India, Cabinet Secretariat Resolution dated the 15th March, 1950 with the Prime Minister as its Chairman. This Resolution required the Planning Commission to:

(1) make an assessment of the material, capital and human resources of the country, including technical personnel, and investigate the possibilities of augmenting such of these resources as are found to be deficient in relation to the nation's requirements;
(2) formulate a plan for the most effective and balanced utilization of the country resources;
(3) as a determination of priorities, define the stages in which the

plan would be carried out and propose the allocation of resources for the due completion of each stage;

(4) indicate the factors which are tending to retard economic development, and determine the conditions which, in view of the current social and political situation, should be established for the successful execution of the plan;

(5) determine the nature of the machinery which will be necessary for securing the successful implementation of each stage of the plan in all its aspects;

(6) appraise from time to time the progress achieved in the execution of each stage of the plan and recommend the adjustments of policy and measures that such appraisal may show to be necessary; and

(7) make such interim or ancillary recommendations as appear to it to be appropriate either for facilitating the discharge of duties assigned to it, or an a consideration of the prevailing economic conditions, current policies, measures and development programmes; or an examination of such specific problems as may be referred to it for advice by Central or State Governments.

1.1. The seven points, as stated above constitute the most concise and comprehensive statement of all conceivable aspects of the planning process imaginable; and the planning at all levels in the country-national, States, district and now Panchayat level has been guided by the processes and principles contained therein. These general principles are purely academic in nature and would guide and govern any rational planning process anytime, anywhere.

2. In para 3 of this Resolution there is a reference to the Directive Principles of State Policy enshrined in the Constitution of India particularly that the state shall strive to promote the welfare of the people by securing and protecting, as effectively as it may, a social order in which justice, social economic and political, shall inform all the institutions of the national life and shall direct its policy towards securing, among other things :

(a) that the citizens, men and women, have the right to an adequate means of livelihood;

(b) that the ownership and control of the material resources of the community are so distributed as best to subserve the common good; and

(c) that the operation of the economic system does not result in the concentration of wealth and means of production to the common detriment.

3. The Planning Commission, conceived and created, as indicated in the Cabinet Secretariat Resolution dated 15th March, 1950 above, greatly contributed to the transformation of the country from an industrially backward economy surviving mostly at subsistence level marginal farming by nearly three-fourths of its teeming millions, to an agricultural surplus and industrially developed country, being reckoned as a major economic power in the world. A Press Note issued on 01 January, 2015, however, without acknowledging this and without giving any reasons, simply said that the Government has replaced Planning Commission with a new institution named NITI Aayog (National Institution for Transforming India). The institution will serve as 'Think Tank' of the Government—a directional and policy dynamo, NITI Aayog will provide Government at the central and state levels with relevant strategic and technical advice across the spectrum of key elements of policy. This includes matters of national and international import on the economic front; dissemination of best practices from within the country as well as from other nations; the infusion of new policy ideas, and specific issue-based support."

4. From the above description, the following points are clear:

(a) NITI Aayog is a new institution and not an improved or modified version of the old and abolished institution known as Planning Commission.
(b) It is new not in the sense of its composition as it is almost similarly constituted as the erstwhile Planning Commission with a Vice Chairman and Members being not only persons of standing in disciplines like economics, sociology, science and technology, or eminent politicians, or those who have excelled in some area of social work, but in the sense that they have the capacity to provide critical inputs of policy and direction to Government at the Central and State levels, particularly in "matters of national and international import on the economic front including infusion of new policy ideas and specific issue-based support".
(c) It is also new in the sense that its functions include

"disseminations of best practices from within the country as well as from other nations."

4.1 The new institution, as conceived, will not be a unit of administration or governance, but a 'Think Tank' of the Government, a "directional and policy dynamo", which will be an "institution" and a "commission", simultaneously, which will "transform" India.

4.2 Transformation literally means many things. It means "changing composition or structure", or changing "outward form or appearance" a changing "character or condition". It may mean all the three kinds of changes, or a combination of any two changes or only one of these changes. But, changes are brought about generally by an executive body, and not a mere 'think tank', which literally means "a body of experts providing advice and ideas on specific political and economic problems". In the Government of India, about every Ministry/Department has a Financial Advisor and other technical advisers also. There is a Chief Economic Advisor and several Economic Advisors in the Ministry of Finance. What would be the position of all such Advisors vis-à-vis NITI Aayog, as they too constitute a 'Think Tank' for the Government to draw upon, whenever needed, is not clear.

5. The author made an application dated 01.05.2018 to the Cabinet Secretariat seeking information u/s 6(1) of the Right to Information Act relating to the Cabinet Resolution dated 1st January, 2015, and also whether consultations were made and approval obtained of representative bodies like the National Development Council, Inter-state Council (with whom recommendations of the Sarkaria Commission relating to Planning Commission were pending consideration), both the Houses of Parliament, Chief Ministers of all the States and UTs and Consultative Committee of the Ministry of Planning (Annexure 16). This applications was transferred to the NITI Aayog by the Cabinet Secretariat u/s 6(3) of the RTI Act, 2005. The salient points which emerge from the information received from NITI Aayog are as follows:

1. "In its 35th Report, on Demand for Grants (2011-12) the Standing Committee on Finance of the 15th Lok Sabha had observed that Planning Commission" has to come to grips with the emerging social realities to reinvent itself to make itself

more relevant and effective for aligning the planning process with economic reforms and its consequences, particularly for the poor."

2. The former Prime Minister, Dr. Manmohan Singh, in his farewell address to the Commission in April, 2014 had raised the following issues :
   (a) The external world is changing rapidly. The structure of the economy and the role of the state in the economy are also changing. With an increasingly open and liberalized economy and a greater reliance on the market mechanism, we need to reflect on what the role of the Planning Commission needs to be in this new world.
   (b) What additional roles should the Planning Commission play and what capacities does it need to build to ensure that it continues to be relevant to the growth process?
   (c) Governance issues being integral to economic growth, are these areas for the Planning Commission to delve into."
3. In para 9 of the 'Note for Cabinet' it is observed that "the Planning Commission is a relic of the era when Central Planning for resource allocation was dominant in development economic philosophy. Most of the countries which adopted centralized state controlled planning and allocation of resources have themselves moved on into newer approaches more suited to the current times."
4. The relations of the Planning Commission with States at times have been acrimonious. There have been concerns that rather than the Finance Commission, the Planning Commission is becoming an arbiter of resource sharing with states resulting in shrinking fiscal space for states and loss of flexibility in implementing their own development programmes.

6. It is significant that in none of the above observations made by Dr. Manmohan Singh and in the Standing Committee Report is there the suggestion that Planning Commission being totally irrelevant, there is a case to abolish or do away with it altogether.

6.1 The Standing Committee of the Lok Sabha observed that it needs "to reinvent itself to make itself more relevant and effective". Dr. Manmohan Singh stressed the "need to reflect" what should be the role of the Planning Commission in an "increasingly open and liberalized economy" and "what capacities it needs to build" to continue to be relevant.

7. There had never been "centralized state controlled planning and allocation of resources" in India in the post-Independence era. Barring a few exceptions made to protect the poor or promote development of basic infra-structure, all prices and consequent resource allocation have been determined by market forces; and both public sector and the private sector have co-existed with the former progressively shrinking and the latter expanding as dictated by the market forces.

7.1 Similarly, the reason for acrimonious relations between the Centre and the States is not the allocation of central assistance by the Planning Commission, which is according to a generally accepted formula known as Gadgil-Mukherjee formula, and additional assistance for externally aided projects, Basic Minimum Services or through centrally sponsored schemes. There could also be no conflict regarding transfer of resources through centrally sponsored schemes. Besides these transfers there is devolution or sharing of tax revenues between the Centre and the States as recommended by the Finance Commission constituted under Article 280 of the Constitution. The States are beneficiaries of these two separate and independent sources of funds; and there could be no scope for any conflict regarding devolution of funds between the Centre and the States or any "shrinking of fiscal space" and "loss of flexibility" for the States "in designing and implementing their own development programmes", as alleged.

8. On the two absolutely invalid grounds mentioned above, viz., "centralized state planning and allocation of resources" and "loss of flexibility in designing and implementing their own development programmes" as outlined above, the Cabinet Note dated 13 August, 2014 initially sought repeal of the Cabinet Secretariat Resolution dated 15th March, 1950 and passing of another such Resolution "establishing the National Development and Reforms Commission (NDRC) for performing functions, which included several planning functions also, like developing "National Development Strategies", "Engaging in Perspective Planning", promoting co-operative federalism" and "Developing methodologies for decentralized planning and decision making". This Cabinet Note had been seen and approved by the Prime Minister. However, as a copy of the Minutes of the Cabinet Meeting in which this Note was considered by the Cabinet sought under the RTI Act has not been made available, there is no way of knowing what

transpired in that meeting and what decision exactly had been taken thereon.

9. NITI Aayog has made available a copy of another Cabinet Note dated 29th December, 2014, which says that "the Cabinet, at its meeting on 13th August, 2014 approved the repeal of the Cabinet Resolution dated 15th March, 1950 .... and authorized the Prime Minister to make such changes as considered necessary in the light of the deliberations on the draft resolution annexed to the Cabinet Note." "Consequent to this decision, the Prime Minister in his address to the nation on 15th August, 2014 outlined the raison d'etre for setting up the new institution."

10. It appears that besides the Cabinet Note dated 13 August, 2014 proposing setting up "National Development and Reforms Commission," there had been another Cabinet Note of the same date proposing establishing a NITI (National Institution for Transforming India) Aayog with a substantially different charter. *Neither a copy of this other Cabinet Note dated 13 August, 2014, nor a copy of the Minutes of the Cabinet Meeting in which it was considered and decision taken on it, have been made available to the author as applied for by him under the RTI Act.* It, however, appears that the Cabinet decision was to repeal the 15th March, 1950 Cabinet Resolution setting up the Planning Commission and replacing it by another Cabinet Resolution dated 1st January, 2015 setting up NITI Aayog, "which would seek to provide a critical directional and strategic input into the development process through its commitment to co-operative federalism, promotion of citizens engagement, egalitarian access to opportunity, participative and adaptive governance and increasing use of technology, besides being the incubator of ideas". These are all very nice phrases : they would also have been practical precepts had it been spelt out which ideas have been inadequately implemented or ignored altogether till now in the last sixty-five years, which would be properly implemented now; and how, and within what time-frame. Without this having been done, these appear to be mere empty words devoid of any practical content.

11. The information received in response to a RTI Query gives a clear indication that it was soon after the announcement on August 15, 2015 by the Prime Minister that "....within a short period, we will replace the planning commission with a new institution...." that the

process of making extensive consultation for designing the new institution was initiated." There had been no such consultation prior to taking the decision to replace the Planning Commission: The subsequent consultation had been consciously restricted to only the design of the new institution which was to replace the Planning Commission. Suggestions were invited on MyGov.in web portal. The portal had a creative corner for suggestions regarding name, logo and taglines of the new institution. Subsequently, on 7th December, 2014, the Prime Minister met the Chief Ministers to elicit their views. There is no indication as to whether any note or write-up or letter had gone to the Chief Ministers spelling out the relevant details of the proposal, giving them time to consider it and meaningfully respond to it. It had been some sort of a monologue by the Prime Minister himself interpreting CMs silence as their consent and considering it to be a complete dialogue resulting in a consensus on the proposed replacement.

12. The papers received in response to the RTI query registration no. PLCOM/R/2018/00121 dated 11/02/2018 also indicate that "Brainstorming Session was organized comprising a wide range of experts/ex-members/eminent persons on 26.8/2014 at Yojna Bhawan. It was held in two separate groups simultaneously comprising eight persons each to seek inputs on the role, functions and structure of the new institution...."

13. Some important points to note about these meetings, of which practically no information is available, are as follows :

(i) There are no names of persons who attended the meetings of these two groups, who chaired them, and whether there was any agenda or agenda notes or specific points for discussion and decision.
(ii) What were the recommendations of these two groups on the above points i.e., role, functions and the structure of the new institution proposed, based on what reasoning or arguments?
(iii) Which recommendations were accepted, and which were rejected and for what reasons?
(iv) Whether the minutes of these meetings, or the points raised and the consensus which emerged in respect of them had been recorded in the form of minutes, and sent to those who attended these meetings, has not been indicated.
(v) The decision to replace the Planning Commission by another

institution had already been taken before this brainstorming session on 26.8.2014. The discussion in these two groups of eight persons each, whose identity has not been disclosed, had presumably been restricted to seeking "inputs on the role, functions and structure of the new institutions." However, no information on these points has been made available in response to the RTI query.

14. The incomplete information received in response to the RTI Query clearly indicates violation of democratic norms and conventions in taking the decision to replace the Planning Commission by NITI Aayog. There is no indication that the matter had been properly taken up with the Chief Ministers of the States and UTs and their views obtained, recorded and duly considered at appropriate level. There is also no indication that the matter was discussed in the meetings of the National Development Council, or the Consultative Committee of the Ministry of Planning or the Parliament.

12

Planning at the Village, District, State and Central Levels Envisaged in the Constitution

The Constitution of India envisages planning and planned development at the village Panchayat, district, State and national levels. This is evident from the following provisions of the Constitution:

1.2 Economic and social, planning has been included as entry no. 20 of List III–Concurrent List of the Seventh Schedule. Article 246 (2) of the Constitution empowers both the Parliament and Legislature of any State exclusively to make laws with respect to any of the matters enumerated in List III of the Seventh Schedule i.e., Concurrent List. The Central Government chose to set up Planning Commission by a Cabinet Resolution. They could have got enacted a law also by the Parliament setting up the Planning Commission.

1.3 Article 40 of the Constitution relating to village panchayat reads as follows:

"The State shall take steps to organize village panchayats and endow them with such powers and authority as may be necessary to enable them to function as units of self-government."

1.4 Besides the above directive, special provisions have been made in the Constitution itself enabling the State legislatures to enact necessary laws to implement this directive.

1.5 The States have set up their own State level planning bodies named as State Planning Commission, State Planning Boards, etc.

1.6 The provisions of the 73rd and 74th Constitution Amendment Acts envisage a three-tier system of Panchayats at the village level, the district level and Intermediate level in the States whose population is above 20 lakhs. Seats in Panchayats at all these three levels shall be filled by direct election from territorial constituencies in the Panchayat area. At the village level, there is Gram Sabha consisting of persons registered in the electoral rolls relating to a village comprised within the area of a Panchayat.

1.7 Planning has thus been mandated by the Constitution of India at all levels from the Gram Panchayat upwards. State legislatures have the legislative power to confer on the Panchayats such powers and authority as may be necessary to enable them to function as institutions of self-government (Articles 243 G and 243 H). They may be entrusted with the responsibility of —

(a) preparing plans of economic development and social justice;
(b) implementation of schemes of economic development and social justice; and
(c) in regard to matters listed in the Eleventh Schedule (inserted by the 73rd Amendment). The list contains 29 items e.g., land improvement, minor irrigation, animal husbandry, fisheries, education, women and child development, etc. The 11th Schedule thus distributes powers between the State Legislature and the Panchayats just as the 7th Schedule distributes powers between the Union and the State Legislatures.

2. It is generally known that India, in the late forties, when it achieved independence from the British rule, was a relatively poor country caught in what Ragner Nurkse in his book 'Problems of Capital Formation in Developing Countries' described as a 'vicious circle of poverty' of low income, low savings, low investment resulting in low incomes again. This process had to be reversed by planned development, increasing incomes and thereby domestic savings, which coupled with help from friendly countries and financial assistance from international lending institutions enabled a developing country like India to invest in major infrastructural projects and reach the "take off" stage from where it soared higher and higher till it became a major agriculturally surplus and industrially developed economy being reckoned as a major economic power. Planning has been playing a steller role in this process of tremendous transformation recognized by all. Without denying it and without any ostensible reason, the Planning Commission was abolished and replaced by an entirely new institution with several novel features, and a name which does not indicate its nature and functions at all: National Institution for

Transforming India Aayog. One could not have imagined a more inappropriate name. The name itself is an eloquent denial of the transformation of a country caught in a "vicious circle of poverty" into an internationally recognized major economic power in the region by its predecessor. The name proclaims it to be an "institution" and "commission" simultaneously. Such an institution will serve as 'Think Tank' of the Government—a directional and policy dynamo" which will provide Government at the Central and State levels with relevant strategic and technical advice across the spectrum of key elements of policy", which "includes matters of national and international import on the economic front, dissemination of best practices from within the country as well as from other nations, the infusion of new policy ideas and specific issue-based support." This description of the nature and functions of this new institution makes it an enigma of both thought and expression, which may possibly amaze and confuse anyone earnestly trying to figure out what it really is about.

3. It is noteworthy that the composition of NITI Aayog is strikingly similar to that of its predecessor — Members and Advisers with similar academic credentials and background and with almost the same supporting staff — but they do not perform any planning functions. They "provide Government at the Central and State levels with relevant strategic and technical advice across the spectrum of key elements of policy". The meaning and content of this function is far from clear; and it may be difficult to indicate even one such advice given by the Aayog during the first four years of the Aayog's existence.

4. Those who have served in the State and the Central Governments at the highest decision making levels know that Government policy is not made everyday; that any entity existing outside the Government (Planning Commission and NITI Aayog also being such entities) can provide policy ideas and inputs only when desired or directed by the Government at the highest levels, and not otherwise, and there cannot conceivably be an organisation outside the Government dictating policies to it. The very idea of a policy dynamo like the NITI Aayog is meaningless unless the intention is to make it openly a part of the Prime Minister's Office. Similarly, the concept of 'Agenda' does not and cannot apply to any Government programme or scheme of development which has to be financed and has certain physical targets to be achieved within a given time limit or time-frame. Any three year programme or action agenda without tieing up or mobilizing the

resources required for its implementation would be a meaningless exercise.

5. The creation of an organization outside the Government as part of NITI Aayog or NITI Aayog itself, to function as a "policy dynamo" "to provide Governments at the Central levels with relevant strategic and technical advice across the spectrum of key elements of policy", without prior meaningful interaction with the concerned Government functionaries, is unimaginable. Such as organization created in India after abolition of the Union Planning Commission has been able to do nothing of the kind in the first four years of its existence: it has only destroyed/disrupted the practical, resource based, realistic planning at the Central, State and sub-state levels, and denied necessary help support, guidance and direction which could have been provided by the erstwhile Planning Commission.

6. The terms "shared vision" and "cooperative federalism" are concepts germane to and part of the planning process. Having abolished the Planning Commission and thereby the mechanism for formulating and monitoring the national and the State Plans, there is no way now for determination of a "shared vision" of all States, and to evolve "cooperative federalism". In the absence of frequent dialogue and interaction between the State and the national level planning bodies, the institution of State Plan Adviser and the concepts of State Plans and their Scheme of Financing as mutually agreed by the representatives of both the State and the Central Planning body, there could be no prospect of there being any "shared vision", and generation of any spirit of "cooperative federalism".

Annexure 1

Excerpts from Speech of the Honourable Prime Minister on August 15, 2014

SECRET

File No. 43011/64/2014-ADMN.1

Government of India

Planning Commission

Annexure-2

"I believe that when Planning Commission was constituted, it was done on the basis of the circumstances and the needs of those times. In recent years, Planning Commission has contributed to the growth of the country in its own way. I respect that, I am proud of that, but the prevalent situation in the country is different, global scenario has also changed, governments are no longer the center of economic activities, the scope of such activities has broadened. State governments have been at the center of development and I consider this a good indication.

If we have to take India forward, it can happen only by taking the states forward. India's federal structure is more important today than in the last 60 years. To strengthen our federal structure, to make our federal structure vibrant, to take our federal structure as a heritage of development, a team of Chief Minister and Prime Minister should be there, a joint team of the Centre and the states should move forward, then to do this job, we will have to think about giving the Planning Commission a look.

So, I am saying from the rampart of the Red Fort that it is a very old system and it will have to be rejuvenated, it will have to be changed a lot. Sometimes it costs more to repair the old house, but, it gives us no satisfaction. Thereafter, we have a feeling that it would be better to construct a new house altogether and therefore within a short period, we will replace the planning commission with a new institution having a new design and structure, a new body, a new soul, a new thinking, a new direction, a new faith towards forging a new direction to lead the country based on creative thinking, public-private partnership, optimum utilisation of resources, utilisation of youth power of the nation, to promote the aspirations of state governments seeking development, to empower the state governments and to empower the federal structure. Very shortly, we are about to move in a direction when this institute would be functioning in place of Planning Commission. "

ANNEXURE-1

SECRET

File No. 43011/64/2014-Admn.1

Government of India

Planning Commission

Annexure 2

P.M.'s Opening Remarks at the Consultation meeting with CMs on replacing the Planning Commission

PM: There is need for a new set-up which will help India take "a big leap forward" in the spirit of cooperative federalism
PM: Need for relook at Planning Commission has been raised since 1992

The Prime Minister, Shri Narendra Modi, today gave a new thrust to the quest for an effective replacement to the Planning Commission, describing "Team India" as a combination of three teams - the Prime Minister and Chief Ministers; the Union Council of Ministers; and the bureaucracy in the Centre and States. He was delivering the opening remarks at a consultation meeting with Chief Ministers on the subject of replacement of the Planning Commission.

Invoking the spirit of "cooperative federalism", the Prime Minister said that the current global scenario offered a chance for India to take a big leap forward. The Prime Minister called for abandoning the incremental approach. He stressed on the need for a suitable body to replace the Planning Commission, so that the strengths of the country can be suitably harnessed.

The Prime Minister said the question of role, relevance and restructuring of the Planning Commission had been repeatedly questioned for more than two decades. The first introspection was done after the launch of economic reforms, in 1992, when it was felt that in light of changing Government policy, a different approach was required. In 2012, the Parliamentary Consultative Committee stressed the need for a serious look at the Planning Commission and the need for a new body to replace it. The former Prime Minister, Dr. Manmohan Singh, had stressed the need for a relook at the Planning Commission towards the end of his term, Shri Narendra Modi added.

Further, the Prime Minister said that when he was Chief Minister of Gujarat, he had attended meetings of the Planning Commission, and had felt the need for a better platform to articulate the view of states. The Prime Minister said that development is now a priority for all, and the time has come to develop a new mechanism to deliver growth and development.

Shri Narendra Modi said it is impossible for the nation to develop unless states develop. He said the process of policy planning also has to change from "top to bottom" to "bottom to top." The Prime Minister also noted that in countries such as the USA, think tanks that function independently of the Government have a major role in policy-making. He said that in India too, there is a great deal of economic activity that happens outside the Government setup, and there is a need to design policies for them as well. He said that states should have a key role in the new body to replace the Planning Commission. He added that states sometimes feel there is no platform to express their views. He also said there should be an effective mechanism to address inter-state disputes.

"Can we develop a new mechanism, that plans according to India's strengths, empowers states, and brings on board all economic activity, including that which happens outside the Government," the Prime Minister asked, as he set the tone for the discussion in today's consultation meeting. He said the views that states express in today's meeting would prove valuable in shaping the new body to replace the Planning Commission.

Annexure 3

Cabinet Resolution dated 01 January, 2015 Replacing Planning Commission with NITI Aayog

Press Information Bureau
Government of India
Cabinet
01-January-2015 17:9 IST
Government constitutes National Institution for Transforming India (NITI) Aayog

Press Note

The Government has replaced Planning Commission with a new institution named NITI Aayog (National Institution for Transforming India). The institution will serve as 'Think Tank' of the Government-a directional and policy dynamo. NITI Aayog will provide Governments at the central and state levels with relevant strategic and technical advice across the spectrum of key elements of policy, this includes matters of national and international import on the economic front, dissemination of best practices from within the country as well as from other nations, the infusion of new policy ideas and specific issue-based support.

The following is the full text of the Cabinet Resolution:

Resolution

Mahatma Gandhi had said: "Constant development is the law of life, and a man who always tries to maintain his dogmas in order to appear consistent drives himself into a false position". Reflecting this spirit and the changed dynamics of the new India, the institutions of governance and policy have to adapt to new challenges and must be built on the founding principles of the Constitution of India, the wealth of knowledge from our civilisational history and the present day socio-cultural context.

2. The Planning Commission was set up on the 15th of March, 1950 through a Cabinet Resolution. Nearly 65 years later, the country has metamorphosed from an under-developed economy to an emergent global nation with one of the world's largest economies.

3. From being preoccupied with survival, our aspirations have soared and today we seek elimination, rather than alleviation, of poverty. The people of India have great expectations for progress and improvement in governance, through their participation. They require institutional reforms

in governance and dynamic policy shifts that can seed and nurture large-scale change. Indeed, the 'destiny' of our country, from the time we achieved Independence, is now on a higher trajectory.

The past few decades have also witnessed a strengthening of Indian nationhood. India is a diverse country with distinct languages, faiths and cultural ecosystems. This diversity has essential or is impracticable".

5. At the heart of the dynamics of transforming India lies a technology revolution and increased access to and sharing of information. In the course of this transformation, while some changes are anticipated and planned, many are a consequence of market forces and larger global shifts. The evolution and maturing of our institutions and polity also entail a diminished role for centralised planning, which itself needs to be redefined.

6. The forces transforming India are many and include:

a. The industry and service sectors have developed and are operating on a global scale now. To build on this foundation, new India needs an administration paradigm in which the government is an "enabler" rather than a "provider of first and last resort". The role of the government as a "player" in the industrial and service sectors has to be reduced. Instead, government has to focus on enabling legislation, policy making and regulation.

b. India's traditional strength in agriculture has increased manifold on account of the efforts of our farmers and improvements in technology. We need to continue to improve, and move from pure food security to a focus on a mix of agricultural production as well as the actual returns that fanners get from their produce.

c. Today, we reside in a 'global village', *connected* by modern transport, communications and media, and networked international markets and institutions. As India 'contributes' to global endeavours, it is also influenced by happenings far removed from our borders. Global economics and geo-politics are getting increasingly integrated, and the private sector is growing in importance as a constituent within that. India needs to be an active player in the debates and deliberations on the global commons, especially in relatively uncharted areas.

d. India's middle class is unique in terms of its size and purchasing power. This formidable group is increasing with the entry of the neo-middle class. It has been an important driver of growth and has enormous potential on account of its high education levels, mobility and willingness to push for change in the country. Our continuing challenge is to ensure that this economically vibrant group remains engaged and its potential is fully realised.

e. India's pool of entrepreneurial, scientific and intellectual human capital is a source of strength waiting to be unleashed to help us attain unprecedented heights of success. In fact, the 'social capital' that is present in our people has been a major contributor to the development of the country thus far and, therefore, it needs to be leveraged through appropriate policy initiatives.
f. The Non-Resident Indian community, which is spread across more than 200 countries, is larger in number than the population of many countries of the world. This is a significant geo-economic and geo-political strength. Future national policies must incorporate this strength in order to broaden their participation in the new India beyond just their financial support. Technology and management expertise are self-evident areas where this community can contribute significantly.
g. Urbanisation is an irreversible trend. Rather than viewing it as an evil, we have to make it an integral part of our policy for development. Urbanisation has to be viewed as an opportunity to use modern technology to create a wholesome and secure habitat while reaping the economic benefits that it offers.
h. Transparency is now a *sine qua non* for good governance. We are in a digital age where the tools and modes of communication, like social media, are powerful instruments to share and explain the thoughts and actions of the government. This trend will only increase with time. Government and governance have to be conducted in an environment of total transparency—using technology to reduce opacity and thereby, the potential for misadventures in governing.

7. Technology and information access have accentuated the unity in diversity that defines us. They have helped integrate different capabilities of our regions, states and eco-systems towards an interlinked national economy. Indeed, Indian nationhood has been greatly strengthened on their account. To reap the benefits of the creative energy that emerges from the Indian kaleidoscope, our development model has to become more consensual and co-operative. It must embrace the specific demands of states, regions and localities. A shared vision of national development has to be worked out based on human dignity, national self-respect and an inclusive and sustainable development path.

8. The challenges we face as a country have also become more complex:

a. India's demographic dividend has to be leveraged fruitfully over the next few decades. The potential of our youth, men and women, has to be realised through education, skill development, elimination of gender bias, and employment. We have to strive to provide our youth productive opportunities to work on the frontiers of science, technology and knowledge economy.

b. Poverty elimination remains one of the most important metrics by which alone we should measure our success as a nation. Every Indian must be given an opportunity to live a life of dignity and self respect. The words of Tiruvalluvar, the sage-poet, when he wrote that "nothing is more dreadfully painful than poverty", and "gripping poverty robs a man of the lofty nobility of his descent", are as true today as they were when written more than two thousand years ago.

c. Economic development is incomplete if it does not provide every individual the right to enjoy the fruits of development. Pt. Deen Dayal Upadhyaya had enunciated this in his concept of Antyodaya, or uplift of the downtrodden, where the goal is to ensure that the poorest of the poor get the benefits of development. Inequalities based on gender biases as well as economic disparities have to be redressed. We need to create an environment and support system that encourages women to play their rightful role in nation-building. Equality of opportunity goes hand in hand with an inclusiveness agenda. Rather than pushing everyone on to a pre-determined path, we have to give every element of society - especially weaker segments like the Scheduled Castes and Scheduled Tribes - the ability to influence the choices the country and government make in setting the national agenda. In fact, inclusion has to be predicated on a belief in the ability of each member of society to contribute. As Sankar Dev wrote centuries ago in the Kirtan Ghosh: "To see every being as equivalent to one's own soul is the supreme means (of attaining deliverance)".

d. Villages *(Gram)* continue to be the bedrock of our ethos, culture and sustenance. They need to be fully integrated institutionally into the development process so that we draw on their vitality and energy.

e. India has more than 50 million small businesses, which are a major source or employment creation. These businesses are particularly important in creating opportunities for the backward and disadvantaged sections of the society. Policy making must focus on providing necessary support to this sector in terms of skill and knowledge upgrades and access to financial capital and relevant technology.

f. Responsible development implies environmentally sound development. India is one of the mega-diverse countries. Our environmental and ecological assets are eternal, and must be preserved and safeguarded. The country's legacy of respect for environment is reflected in our reverence for trees and animals. Our legacy to future generations must be sustainable progress. Each element of our environment *(paryavaran)* and resources, namely water, land and forest *(Jed, Jameen evam Jungle)* must be protected; and this must be done in a manner that takes into account their inter-linkages with climate *(jal vayu)* and people *(Jan)*. Our development agenda has to ensure that development does not sully the quality of life of the present and future generations.

9. The role of the government in achieving 'national objectives' may change with time, but will always remain significant. Government will continue to set policies that anticipate and reflect the country's requirements and execute them in a just manner for the benefit of the citizens. The continuing integration with the world - politically and economically - has to be incorporated into policy making as well as functioning of the government.

In essence, effective governance in India will rest on the following pillars:

a. **Pro-people agenda** that fulfils the aspirations of the society as well as individual,
b. **Pro-active** in anticipating and responding to their needs,
c. **Participative,** by involvement of citizens,
d. **Empowering** women in all aspects
e. **Inclusion** of all groups, with special attention to the economically weak *(garib),* the SC, ST and OBC communities, the rural sector and farmers *(gaon and kisan),* youth and all categories of minorities.
f. **Equality of opportunity** to our country's youth,
g. **Transparency** through the use of technology to make government visible and responsive.

10. Governance, across the public and private domains, is the concern of society as a whole. Everyone has a stake in ensuring good governance and effective delivery of services. Creating Jan Chetna, therefore, becomes crucial for people's initiative. In the past, governance may have been rather narrowly construed as public governance. In today's changed dynamics - with 'public' services often being delivered by 'private' entities, and the greater scope for 'participative citizenry', governance encompasses and involves everyone.

11. The institutional framework of government has developed and matured over the years. This has allowed the development of domain expertise which allows us the chance to increase the specificity of functions given to institutions. Specific to the planning process, there is a need to

separate as well as energize the distinct 'process' of governance from the 'strategy' of governance.

In the context of governance structures, the changed requirements of our country, point to the need for setting up an institution that serves as a Think Tank of the government - a directional and policy dynamo. The proposed institution has to provide governments at the central and state levels with relevant strategic and technical advice across the spectrum of key elements of policy. This includes matters of national and international import on the economic front, dissemination of best practices from within the country as well as from other nations, the infusion of new policy ideas and specific issue-based support. The institution has to be able to respond to the changing and more integrated world that India is part of.

An important evolutionary change from the past will be replacing a centre-to-state one-way flow of policy by a genuine and continuing partnership with the states. The institution must have the necessary resources, knowledge, skills and, ability to act with speed to provide the strategic policy vision for the government as well as deal with contingent issues.

Perhaps most importantly, the institution must adhere to the tenet that while incorporating positive influences from the world, no single model can be transplanted from outside into the Indian scenario. We need to find our own strategy for growth. The new institution has to zero in on what will work in and for India. It will be a Bharatiya approach to development.

12. The institution to give life to these aspirations is the **NITI Aayog (National Institution for** Transforming India). This is being proposed after extensive consultation across the spectrum of stakeholders including *inter alia* state governments, domain experts and relevant institutions. The NITI Aayog will work towards the following objectives:

a. To evolve a shared vision of national development priorities, sectors and strategies with the active involvement of States in the light of national objectives. The vision of the NITI Aayog will then provide a framework 'national agenda' for the Prime Minister and the Chief Ministers to provide impetus to.
b. To foster cooperative federalism through structured support initiatives and mechanisms with the States on a continuous basis, recognising that strong States make a strong nation.
c. To develop mechanisms to formulate credible plans at the village level and aggregate these progressively at higher levels of government.
d. To ensure, on areas that are specifically referred to it, that the interests of national security are incorporated in economic strategy and policy.

e. To pay special attention to the sections of our society that may be at risk of not benefitting adequately from economic progress.
f. To design strategic and long term policy and programme frameworks and initiatives, and monitor their progress and their efficacy. The lessons learnt through monitoring and feedback will be used for making innovative improvements, including necessary mid-course corrections.
g. To provide advice and encourage partnerships between key stakeholders and national and international like-minded Think Tanks, as well as educational and policy research institutions.
h. To create a knowledge, innovation and entrepreneurial support system through a collaborative community of national and international experts, practitioners and other partners.
i. To offer a platform for resolution of inter-sectoral and inter-departmental issues in order to accelerate the implementation of the development agenda.
j. To maintain a state-of-the-art Resource Centre, be a repository of research on good governance and best practices in sustainable and equitable development as well as help their dissemination to stake-holders.
k. To actively monitor and evaluate the implementation of programmes and initiatives, including the identification of the needed resources so as to strengthen the probability of success and scope of deliver''.
1. To focus on technology upgradation and capacity building for implementation of programmes and initiatives.
m. To undertake other activities as may be necessary in order to further the execution of the national development agenda, and the objectives mentioned above.

13. The NITI Aayog will comprise the following:

a. Prime Minister of India as the Chairperson
b. Governing Council comprising the Chief Ministers of all the States and Lt. Governors of Union Territories
c. Regional Councils will be formed to address specific issues and contingencies impacting more than one state or a region. These will be formed for a specified tenure. The Regional Councils will be convened by the Prime Minister and will comprise of the Chief Ministers of States and Lt. Governors of Union Territories in the region. These will be chaired by the Chairperson of the NITI Aayog or his nominee.

d. Experts, specialists and practitioners with relevant domain knowledge as special invitees nominated by the Prime Minister
e. The full-time organisational framework will comprise of, in addition to the Prime Minister as the Chairperson:
    i. Vice-Chairperson: To be appointed by the Prime Minister
    ii. Members: Full-time
    iii. Part-time members: Maximum of 2 from leading universities research organisations and other relevant institutions in an ex-officio capacity. Part time members will be on a rotational basis.
    iv. Ex-Officio members: Maximum of 4 members of the Union Council of Ministers to be nominated by the Prime Minister.
    v. Chief Executive Officer: To be appointed by the Prime Minister for a fixed tenure, in the rank of Secretary to the Government of India.
    vi. Secretariat as deemed necessary.

14. Swami Vivekananda said "Take up one idea. Make that one idea your life - think it, dream of it, live on that idea. Let the brain, muscles, nerves, every part of your body, be full of that idea and just leave every other idea alone. This is the way to success." Through its commitment to a cooperative federalism, promotion of citizen engagement, egalitarian access to opportunity, participative and adaptive governance and increasing use of technology, the NITI Aayog will seek to provide a critical directional and strategic input into the development process. This, along with being the incubator of ideas for development, will be the core mission of NITI Aayog.

Cabinet Secretariat. Government of India

Annexure 4

Government of India's Resolution dated 15th March, 1950 Setting up the Planning Commission

'Government of India
Cabinet Secretariat'
Resolution
(Planning)

New Delhi, the 15th March, 1950

No.1-P(C)/50—For some years past, the people of India have been conscious of the importance of planned development as a means of raising the country's standard of living. This consciousness found expression in the appointment in 1938 of the National Planning Committee by the Indian National Congress. The work of the Committee was, however, interrupted by political and other developments in the beginning of the war, although much useful material has since been published. In 1944, the Government of India established a separate Department of Planning and Development and at its instance, the Central as well as the Provincial Governments prepared a number of development schemes to be undertaken after the war. Problems of planning were reviewed towards the end of 1949 by the Advisory Planning Board which was appointed by the Interim Government of India, an important recommendation of the Board being the appointment of a Planning Commission to devote continuous attention to the whole field of development, so far as the Central Government was concerned with it.

2. During the last three years, the Centre as well as the Provinces have initiated schemes of development, but experience has shown that progress has been hampered by the absence of adequate co-ordination and of sufficiently precise information about the availability of resources With the integration of the former Indian States with the rest of country and the emergence of new geographical and economic facts, a fresh assessment of the financial and other resources and of the essential conditions of progress has now become necessary. Moreover, inflationary pressures inherited from the war, balance of payments difficulties, the influx into India of several million persons displaced from their homes and occupations, deficiencies in the country's food supply aggravated by partition and a succession of indifferent harvests, and the dislocation of supplies of certain essential raw materials have placed the economy under a severe strain. The need

for comprehensive planning based on a careful appraisal of resources and on an objective analysis of all the relevant economic factors has become imperative. These purposes can best be achieved through an organisation free from the burden of the day-to-day administration, but in constant touch with the Government at the highest policy level. Accordingly, as announced by the Honourable Finance Minister in his Budget speech on the 28th February, 1950, the Government of India have decided to set up a Planning Commission.

3. The Constitution of India has guaranteed certain Fundamental Rights to the citizens of India and enunciates certain Directive Principles of State Policy, in particular, that the State shall strive to promote the welfare of the people by securing and protecting as effectively as it may a social order in which justice, social economic and political, shall inform all the institutions of the national life and shall direct its policy towards securing, among other things:

(a) that the citizens, men and women, equally, have the right to an adequate means of livelihood;
(b) that the ownership and control of the material resources of the community are so distributed as best to subserve the common good; and
(c) that the operation of the economic system does not result in the concentration of wealth and means of production to the common detriment.

4. Having regard to these rights and in furtherance of these principles as well as of the declared objective of the Government to promote a rapid rise in the standard of living of the people by efficient exploitation of the resources of the country, increasing production, and offering opportunities to all for employment in the service of the community.

The Planning Commission will:

1. make an assessment of the material, capital and human resources of the country, including technical personnel, and investigate the possibilities of augmenting such of these resources as are found to be deficient in relation to the nation's requirements;
2. formulate a Plan for the most effective and balanced utilisation of the country's resources;
3. on a determination of priorities, define the stages in which the Plan should be carried out and propose the allocation of resources for the due completion of each stage;
4. indicate the factors which are tending to retard economic development, and determine the conditions which, in view of the

current social and political situation, should be established for the successful execution of the Plan:

5. determine the nature of the machinery which will be necessary for securing the successful implementation of each stage of the Plan in all its aspects;
6. appraise from time to time the progress achieved in the execution of each stage of the Plan and recommend the adjustments of policy and measures that such appraisal may show to be necessary; and
7. make such interim or ancillary recommendations as appear to it to be appropriate either for facilitating the discharge of the duties assigned to it, or on a consideration of the prevailing economic conditions, current policies, measures and development programmes; or on an examination of such specific problem as may be referred to it for advice by Central or State Governments.

5. The Planning Commission will be composed of the following:

Chairman	:	Shri Jawaharlal Nehru
Deputy Chairman	:	Shri Gulzarilal Nanda
Members	:	Shri V.T. Krishnamachari
	:	Shri Chintaman Deshmukh
	:	Shri G.L. Mehta Shri R.K. Patil
Secretary:	:	Shri N.R. Pillai
Deputy Secretary	:	Shri Tarlok Singh

6. The Planning Commission will make recommendations to the Cabinet. In framing its recommendations, the Commission will act in close understanding and consultation with the Ministries of the Central Government and the Governments of the States. The responsibility for taking and implementing decisions will rest with the Central and the State Governments. The Government of India feel confident that the States will give the fullest measure of help to the Commission, so as to ensure the maximum coordination in policy and unity in effort.

7. The work of the Planning Commission will affect decisively the future welfare of the people in every sphere of national life. Its success will depend on the extent to which it enlists the association and cooperation of the people at all levels. The Government of India, therefore, earnestly hope that in carrying out its task the Commission will receive the maximum support and goodwill from all interests and in particular, from industry and labour.

8. The headquarters of the Commission will be at New Delhi.

Annexure 5

Press Information Bureau, Government of India, NITI Aayog: Significant Achievements of NITI Aayog Over the Last Three Years

Press Information Bureau
Government of India
NITI Aayog

22-April-2017 17:311ST

I. Vision Document, Strategy & Action Agenda beyond 12th Five Year Plan

Replacing the Five Year Plans beyond 31st March, 2017. NITI Aayog is in the process of preparing the 15-year vision document keeping in view the social goals set and/ or proposed for a period of 15 years; A 7-year strategy document spanning 2017-18 to 2023-24 to convert the longer-term vision into implementable policy and action as a part of a "National Development Agenda" is also being worked upon. The 3-year Action Agenda for 2017-18 to 2019-20, aligned to the predictability of financial resources during the 14th Finance Commission Award period, has been completed and will be submitted before the Prime Minister on April 23rd at the 3rd Governing Council Meeting.

II. Reforms in Agriculture

a. Model Land Leasing Law

Taking note of increasing incidents of leasing in and out of land and suboptimal use of land with lesser number of cultivators, NITI Aayog has formulated a Model Agricultural Land Leasing Act, 2016 to both recognize the rights of the tenant and safeguard interest of landowners A dedicated cell for land reforms was also set up in NITI Based on the model act, Madhya Pradesh has enacted separate land leasing law and Uttar Pradesh and Uttarakhand have modified their land leasing laws. Some States, including Odisha, Andhra Pradesh and Telangana, are already at an advance stage of formulating legislations to enact their land leasing laws for agriculture.

b. Reforms of the Agricultural Produce Marketing Committee Act

NITI Aayog consulted with the States on 21 October 2016 on three critical reforms :

(i) Agricultural marketing reforms
(ii) Felling and transit laws for tree produce grown at private land
(iii) Agricultural land leasing

Subsequently, Model APMC Act version 2 prepared. States are being consulted to adopt APMC Act version 2.

c. Agricultural Marketing and Farmer Friendly Reforms Index

NITI Aayog has developed the first ever 'Agriculture Marketing and Farmer Friendly Reforms Index' to sensitise states about the need to undertake reforms in the three key areas of Agriculture Market Reforms, Land Lease Reforms and Forestry on Private Land (Felling and Transit of Trees). The index carries a score with a minimum value "0" implying no reforms and maximum value "100" implying complete reforms in the selected areas.

As per NITI Aayog's index, Maharashtra ranks highest in implementation of various agricultural reforms. The State has implemented most of the marketing reforms and offers the best environment for undertaking agri-business among all the States and UTs. Gujarat ranks second with a score of 71.50 out of 100, closely followed by Rajasthan and Madhya Pradesh, Almost two-third States have not been able to reach even the halfway mark of reforms score, in the year 2016-17. The index aims to induce a healthy competition between States and percolate best practices in implementing farmer-friendly reforms.

III. Reforming Medical Education

A committee chaired by Vice Chairman, NITI Aayog recommended scrapping of the Medical Council of India suggested a new body for regulating medical education. The draft legislation for the proposed National Medical Commission has been submitted to the Government for further necessary action.

IV. Digital Payments Movement

a. An action plan on advocacy, awareness and co-ordination of handholding efforts among general public, micro enterprises and other stakeholders was prepared. Appropriate literature in print and multimedia was prepared on the subject for widespread dissemination. Presentations/ interactions were organised by NITI Aayog for training and capacity building of various Ministries/ Departments of Government of India, representatives of State/UTs, Trade and Industry Bodies as well as all other stakeholders.

b. NITI Aayog also constituted a Committee of Chief Ministers on Digital Payments on 30th November 2016 with the Chief Minister of Andhra Pradesh, Chandrababu Naidu, as the Convener to promote transparency, financial inclusion and a healthy financial ecosystem nationwide. The Committee submitted its interim report to Hon'ble Prime Minister in January 2017.
c. To incentivize the States/UTs for promotion of digital transactions, Central assistance of Rs. 50 crore would be provided to the districts for undertaking Information, Education and Communication activities to bring 5 crore Jan Dhan accounts to digital platform.
d. Cashback and referral bonus schemes were launched by the Prime Minister on 14.4.2017 to promote the use of digital payments through the BHIM App.
e. Niti Aayog also launched two incentive schemes to promote digital payments across all sections of society the Lucky Grahak Yojana and the Digi Dhan Vyapar Yojana—Over 16 lakh consumers and merchants have won Rs. 256 crore under these two schemes.
f. Digi Dhan Melas were also held for 100 days in 100 cities, from December 25th to April 14th.

V. Atal Innovation Mission

The Government has set up Atal Innovation Mission (AIM) in NITI Aayog with a view to strengthen the country's innovation and entrepreneurship ecosystem by creating institutions and programs that spur innovation in schools, colleges, and entrepreneurs in general. In 2016-17, the following major schemes were rolled out:

a. Atal Tinkering Labs (ATLs): To foster creativity and scientific temper in students, AIM is helping to establish 500 ATLs in schools across India, where students can design and make small prototypes to solve challenges they see around them, using rapid prototyping technologies that have emerged in recent years.
b. Atal Incubation Centres (AICs): AIM will provide financial support of Rs. 10 crore and capacity buidling for setting AICs across India, which will help startups expand quicker and enable innovation-entrepreneurship, in core sectors such as manufacturing, transport, energy, education, agriculture, water and sanitation, etc.

VI. Indices Measuring States' Performance in Health, Education and Water Management

As part of the Prirm Minister's Focus on outcomes, NITI has come out with indices to measure incremental annual outcomes in critical social sectors like health, education and water with a view to nudge the states into competing with each other for better outcomes, while at the same time sharing best practices & innovations to help each other - an example of competitive and cooperative federalism.

VII. Sub-Group of Chief Ministers on Rationalisation of Centrally Sponsored Schemes

Based on the recommendations of this Sub-Group, a Cabinet note was prepared by NITI Aayog which was approved by the Cabinet on 3rd August, 2016. Among several key decision, the sub-group led to the rationalisation of the existing CSSs into 28 umbrella schemes.

VIII. Sub-Group of Chief Ministers on Swachh Bharat Abhiyan

Constituted by NITI Aayog on 9th March, 2015, the Sub-Group has submitted its report to the Hon'ble Prime Minister in October, 2015 and most of its recommendations have been accepted.

IX. Sub-Group of Chief Ministers on Skill Development

Constituted on 91 March, 2015, the report of the Sub-Group of Chief Ministers on Skill Development was presented before the Hon'ble Prime Minister on 31/12/2015. The recommendation and actionable points emerging from the Report were approved by the Hon'ble Prime Minister and are in implementation by the Ministry of Skill Development

X. Task Force on Elimination of Poverty in India

Constituted on 16th March, 2015 under the Chairmanship of Dr. Arvind Panagariya, Vice Chairman, NITI Aayog, the report of the Task Force was finalised and submitted to the Prime Minister on 11 July, 2016. The report of the Task Force primarily focusses on issues of measurement of poverty and strategies to combat poverty. Regarding estimation of poverty, the report of the Task Force states that "a consensus in favour of either the Tendulkar or a higher poverty line did not emerge. Therefore, the Task Force has concluded that the matter be considered in greater depth by the country's top experts on poverty before a final decision is made. Accordingly, it is recommended that an expert committee be set up to arrive at an informed decision on the level at which the poverty line should be set." With respect to strategies to combat poverty, the Task Force has made recommendations on faster poverty reduction through employment intensive sustained rapid growth and effective implementation of anti-poverty programs.

XI. Task Force on Agriculture Development

The Task Force on Agricultural development was constituted on 16th March, 2015 under the Chairmanship of Dr. Arvind Panagariya, Vice Chairman, NITI Aayog. The Task Force based on its works prepared an occasional paper entitled "Raising Agricultural Productivity and Making Farming Remunerative for Farmers" focusing on 5 critical areas of Indian Agriculture. These are (i) Raising Productivity, (ii) Remunerative Prices to Farmers, (iii) Land Leasing, Land Records & Land Titles; (iv) Second Green Revolution-Focus on Eastern States; and (v) Responding to Farmers' Distress. After taking inputs of all the States on occasional paper and through their reports, the Task Force submitted the final report to Prime Minister on 31st May, 2016. It has suggested important policy measures to bring in reforms in agriculture for the welfare of the farmers as well as enhancing their income.

XII. Transforming India Lecture Series

As the government's premier think-tank, NITI Aayog views knowledge building & transfer as the enabler of real transformation in States. To build knowledge systems for States and the Centre, NITI Aayog launched the 'NITI Lectures: Transforming India' series, with full support of the Prime Minister on 26th August, 2016. The lecture series is aimed at addressing the top policy making team of the Government of India, including members of the cabinet and several top layers of the bureaucracy. It aims is to bring cutting edge ideas in development policy to Indian policy makers and public, so as to promote the cause of transformation of India into a prosperous modern economy. The Deputy Prime Minister of Singapore, Shri Tharman Shanmugaratnam, delivered the first lecture on the topic: India and the Global Economy. On November 16th, 2016, Bill Gates, Co-Founder, Bill and Melinda Gates Foundation, delivered the second lecture in the series under the theme: 'Technology and Transformation'.

Annexure 6

The Three Years Action Agenda

Published by NITI Aayog Sansad Marg,
New Delhi
www.niti.gov.in

The Three Year Action Agenda, a NITI Aayog document, is based on extensive discussions with and inputs from the central ministries and State governments. The Governing Council of the NITI Aayog, consisting of the Prime Minister as its Chairperson and several Union Ministers and State Chief Ministers as Members, extensively deliberated on the document in its draft form at its meeting on 23rd April 2017. This final document incorporates the comments made at the meeting and those received subsequently from Chief Ministers.

Preface

On 1st January 2015, the National Institution for Transforming India or NITI Aayog came into existence as the government's premier think tank. Subsequently, vide Office Order PMO ID No. 360/31/C/38/2014-ES-I1 dated 09/05/2016 (Annexure 1), the Prime Minister's Office advised the NITI Aayog to prepare Fifteen Year Vision, Seven Year Strategy and Three Year Action Agenda documents. Accordingly, the present document is being published to recommend policy changes and programmes for action from 2017-18 to 2019-20, the last three years of the Fourteenth Finance Commission. A second document containing the Fifteen Year Vision and Seven Year Strategy is currently under preparation at the NITI Aayog.

The Vision, Strategy and Action Agenda exercise represents a departure from the Five Year Plan process, followed with a handful of discontinuities until the fiscal year 2016-17. The 12th Five Year Plan was the last of these plans. It has been felt that with an increasingly open and liberalised economy, we needed to rethink the tools and approaches to conceptualising the development process. The proposed shift represents an important step in this direction.

The Action Agenda has been prepared as an integral part of the exercise leading to the Vision and Strategy document. It has been fast tracked and released first, keeping in view that with the start of fiscal year 2016-17, it is of immediate relevance for policy implementation. Work on the Vision and Strategy document is already far advanced.

The Three Year Action Agenda offers ambitious proposals for policy changes within a relatively short period. It is understood that while some may be fully implemented during the three-year period, implementation of others would continue into the subsequent years. Where relevant, we have included possible actions by the states to complement the efforts of the Centre.

For holistic development, all ministries and departments must progress simultaneously and harmoniously. Therefore, as a roadmap for future progress, the Action Agenda attempts to cover nearly all aspects of the economy. Despite this wide coverage, an effort has been made to present all action points with the utmost clarity. To ensure that the document does not become unduly long, however, we have deliberately refrained from providing the detailed rationale for each proposed action Where appropriate and necessary, we propose to undertake this latter task in the Vision and Strategy document.

The Action Agenda is the result of the had work and efforts of a vast number of individuals and institutions. The NITI Aayog has been lucky to have three world-renowned scholars as its Members: Shri Bibek Debroy, Dr. V.K. Saraswat and Dr. Ramesh Chand. It also has a number of outstanding Advisers leading its work in different areas of policy working under the guidance of the Members, the Advisers and their teams prepared the core inputs that formed the backbone of the final document. I greatly appreciate the contributions of the Members, Advisers and their teams to the Action Agenda.

Inputs were also sought and received from State Governments, Union Territories and Ministries of the Central Government. Extensive consultations were held with groups of scientists, economists, journalists, voluntary organisations, industry associations and experts in education, health, culture, transport and other fields. Many outside experts also provided extremely useful written inputs. Annexure 2 at the end of the document lists the outside experts exhaustively with the hope that I have not missed anyone. I sincerely thank the states, union territories, Ministries, outside experts and institutions for the gift of their ideas and time.

Shri Amitabh Kant, the Chief Executive Officer of the NITI Aayog, skilfully steered the entire process to its logical conclusion. The task simply could not have been completed without his leadership in navigating and guiding all those involved throughout die process. I am deeply appreciative of the energy and time he generously provided.

A dedicated team of six talented young policy analysts, who recently joined the NITI Aayog, worked under my close direction to convert the inputs provided by die Advisers and outside experts into a unified document. They are: Chinmaya Goyal, Atisha Kumar, Urvashi Prasad, Vaibhav Kapoor, Rahul Ahluwalia and Devashish Dhar. This part of the exercise consisted of preparation of different chapters, fitting them into a single whole and revising the draft multiple times. The process also included several discussions lasting hours. Atisha and Chinmaya jointly performed the key functions of coordination and editing of the document throughout the process. It was a real pleasure for me working with this brilliant, energetic and enthusiastic team of young analysts.

Pavithra Rangan oversaw the publication and production of" the document. My office staff, headed by Dr. Prem Singh, provided critical logistical support. Prem not only saw to it that all went smoothly but also provided critical intellectual inputs at all stages of the work.

In draft form, the Action Agenda was circulated to all members of the Governing Council of the NITI Aayog at its third meeting on 23rd April, 2017. Subsequently, several states and their Chief Ministers provided comments on that draft document. A concerted effort has been made to incorporate these inputs as well as the remarks made by the Chief Ministers at the Governing Council meeting in this final version.

It is hoped that the Three Year Action Agenda will help launch a new phase in our journey towards a New India.

New Delhi — **Arvind Panagariya**
1 August, 2017 — Vice Chairman

CHAPTER 1:
Three Year Action Agenda: An Overview

1.1. The objective of eliminating poverty in all its dimensions such that every citizen has access to a minimum standard of food, education, health, clothing, shelter, transportation and energy has been at the heart of India's development efforts since Independence. The extremely low level of per-capita income and widespread poverty made it impossible for us to achieve this objective without growing the economy. Tax revenues were so meagre and the economy's needs so vast that no serious dent into poverty could be made through redistribution alone. While we substantially improved economic performance during the first four decades of independence over that during the preceding fifty years, growth remained below 4%, which was woefully inadequate for a meaningful decline in poverty.

1.2. But the signs of change began to emerge during die second half of the 1980s, with 1991 proving to be a turning point. The reforms that followed first under Prime Minister Narasimha Rao and then under Prime Minister Atal Bihari Vajpayee placed India first on a 6% growth trajectory and then, beginning in 2003-04, on an 8% plus trajectory. Rising wages accompanied faster growth and pulled many out of abject poverty. Growth also yielded handsome gains in tax revenues, which helped expand social spending manifold, reinforcing the direct effect of growth on poverty reduction.

1.3. Although a combination of global economic developments and domestic policy choices led to a dip in the growth rate to 5.6% in 2012-13; quick corrective action in 2014. followed by sustained policy reforms, has helped the economy sustain 7% plus growth during the three years ending on 31 March 2017. Indeed, there are good prospects that we will return to the 8% plus growth trajectory in another two to three years if not sooner. Therefore, the chances of a massive cut in the poverty rate in the upcoming decade are excellent.

1.4. India's 125 Crore citizens, a majority of which consists of the youth, increasingly aspire for greater empowerment and a better quality of life. It is in recognition of these joint aspirations hat the Prime Minister has called for the transformation of India with the "Participation of All and Development of All" or "Sabka Saath, Sabka Vikas."

1.5. In this backdrop, the present document charts an ambitious, transformational yet achievable Action Agenda for the government during 2017-18 to 2019-20, that constitute the last three years of the Fourteenth Finance Commission. The Agenda is a part of a longer-term Fifteen-year Vision and Seven-year Strategy outlined in a separate document. The Action Agenda proposes a path to achieve all-round development of India and its people. A brief outline of the subject's covered in *the* document is provided below.

Part I: Medium-Term Revenue and Expenditure Framework

1.6. The most direct and visible policy tool of the government is the budget. The allocation of expenditure needs to be aligned to the government's overall objectives. Accordingly, chapters 2-4 in Part I present expenditure proposals for three years based on revenue forecasts'. This exercise has been limited to the Central government.

1.7. During the past three years (2014-15 to 2016-17), the government has made significant progress towards implementing a sound and stable fiscal strategy. The fiscal deficit has been cut from 4.5% of the Gross Domestic Product (GDP) in 2013-14 to 3.5% in 2016-17 while the revenue deficit has been reduced from 3.2% to 2.1% of die GDP over the same period. It is proposed that the government should capitalize on this progress by maintaining its course during the next three years. Under the proposed fiscal framework, the fiscal deficit is to be reduced to its eventual target of 3% of the GDP under the Fiscal Responsibility and Budget Management (FRBM) framework by 2018-19, while the revenue deficit is expected to fall to 0.9% of the GDP by 2019-20.

1.8. The Action Agenda proposes linking Central government expenditures to future priorities. It suggests shifting the composition of expenditures by allocating a larger proportion of additional revenues that become available over time to high-priority sectors. Under the proposed agenda, the share of non-developmental revenue expenditure in total expenditure would decline from 47% in 2015-16 to 41% in 2019-20. At the same time, the share of capital expenditure, which is more likely to promote development, would rise significantly. The proposals imply substantial expansion in expenditures by 2019-20 on education, health, agriculture, rural development, defence, railways, roads and other categories of capital expenditure.

Part II: Economic Transformations in Major Sectors

1.9. This part includes two chapters, one dealing with agriculture, which is die backbone of the rural economy, and the other focuses on industry and services in which die key issue is the creation of well-paid jobs.

Agriculture: Doubling Farmers' Incomes

1.10.Farmers make up nearly half of India's workforce. Therefore, for India to flourish, its farmers and the farm economy must prosper. It is against this background that the Prime Minister has called for doubling farmers' incomes by 2022. To achieve this goal, the Action Agenda onlines a strong programme for agricultural transformation. It includes numerous measures to raise farm productivity, bring remunerative prices to farmers, put farmers' land to productive uses when they are not able to farm it themselves and improve the implementation of relief measures. Chapters in subsequent parts of the document offer an ambitious agenda for empowering the rural population through improved road and digital connectivity, access to clean energy, financial inclusion and "Housing for All."

1.11. Enhancing agricultural productivity requires of" efficiently using inputs, introducing new technologies and shifting from low to high value commodities. We need to expand the scope of irrigation to increase crop intensity, improve access to irrigation, enhance the seed replacement rate and encourage the balanced use of fertilizers. Precision farming and related new technologies, that allow highly efficient farming and conserve resources, must be spread through appropriate policy interventions. Conditions conducive to shift into high value commodities such as horticulture, dairying, poultry, piggery, small ruminant husbandry, fisheries and forestry need to be created.

1.12. The reform of the Agricultural Produce Marketing Committees (APMC) Act needs a new lease of life. Farmers should get genuine rights for direct sales to buyers of all commodities, potential buyers should get the rights to buy produce directly from farmers, entry of private agricultural markets should be free and an effective legal framework for contract farming should be established. Minimum Support Prices (MSPs) have distorted cropping patterns clue to their use in certain commodities in selected regions. There has been an excessive focus on the procurement of wheat, rice and sugarcane at the expense of other crops such as pulses, oilseed and coarse grains. These distortions have led to the depletion of water resources, soil degradation and deterioration in water quality in the North-west. At the same time, eastern states, where procurement at the MSP is minimal or non-existent, have suffered. One measure that can help reduce distortions in the MSP system is the system of "Price Deficiency Payment." While MSP may still be used for need-based procurement, under the deficiency payments system, a subsidy may be provided to farmers on other targeted produce, contingent on prices falling below an MSP-linked direshold,

1.13. Over the years, landholdings in India have become smaller and fragmented. According to die 2010-11 Agricultural Census, 47% of landholdings had become less than half a hectare in size. These holdings are too small to support a family of five so that many farmers now seek alternative sources of income. But stringent tenancy laws in most states have meant that these farmers hesitate to lease the land they leave behind. As a result, an increasing amount of farmland is being left fallow. The introduction of a modern land-leasing law that balances and protects the rights of the tenant and landowners would be a potential solution.

1.14. Finally, to alleviate distress in case of natural calamities, the government has recently introduced the Fasal Bima Yojana. This is an important positive step toward mitigating risk but requires improvement. Capping the subsidy amount per farm household to a fixed amount and charging the full premium for additional insurance would not only economize on financial resources but will also be more equitable.

Trade, Industry and Services: Creating Well-Paid Jobs

1.15.Contrary to some assertions that India's growth has been "jobless," the Employment Unemployment Surveys (EUS) of the National Sample Survey Office (NSSO), which till date remain the most reliable sources of information on India's employment situation, have consistently reported low and stable rates of unemployment over more man three decades. Even under the most demanding definition of employment, the unemployment rate consistently remains between 5% and 8%.

1.16. Indeed, unemployment is the lesser of India's problems. The more serious problem, instead, is severe underemployment. A job that one worker can perform is often performed by two or more workers. In effect, those in die workforce are employed, but they are overwhelmingly stuck in low-productivity, low-wage jobs.

1.17. Three examples illustrate the point. First, in 2011-12, as per the NSSO Employment Unemployment Survey, 49% of the workforce was employed in agriculture. But agriculture contributed only 17% of India's GDP at current prices. Second, in 2010-11, firms with less than 20 workers employed 72% of India's manufacturing workforce but contributed only 12% of manufacturing output2. Finally, services are no different. According to the 2006-07 NSSO survey of service firms, the 650 largest enterprises accounted for 38% of services output but only employed 2% of services workers. Put another way, the remaining services firms employed 98% of the workforce but produced only 62% of the output.

1.18. Therefore, what is needed is the creation of high-productivity, high-wage jobs. Accordingly, Chapter 6 of the Action Agenda focuses on the measures necessary for the increased emergence of larger, organised-sector firms. The experience of countries that managed to transform rapidly, such as South Korea, Taiwan, Singapore and China, shows that the manufacturing sector and the ability to compete in the vast global marketplace hold the key to the creation of well-paid jobs for low and semi-skilled workers. The "Make in India" campaign needs to succeed by manufacturing for global markets.

1.19. A focus on the domestic market through an import-substitution strategy, however, attractive it may seem, would give rise to a group of relatively small firms behind a high wall of protection. They will not only fail to exploit scale economies but also miss out on productivity gains that come from competing against the best in the world. The electronics industry offers a case in point. Our domestic market in electronics as of 2015 is only USD 65 billion. In contrast, the global market is USD 2 trillion. Our policy of import substitution under high protection has given rise to a group of small firms none of which is competitive in the world markets. In contrast, a focus on the global market can potentially result in output worth hundreds of billions of dollars and hence a large number of well-paid jobs.

1.20. Today, with Chinese wages rising wages due to an ageing workforce, many large-scale firms in labour-intensive sectors currently manufacturing in that country are looking for lower-wage locations. With its large workforce and competitive wages, India would be a natural home for these firms. Therefore, the time for adopting a manufactures and exports-based strategy could not be more opportune. Keeping this context in view; the Action Agenda offers detailed proposals for the implementation of an exports-based strategy. Among other things, it recommends the creation of a handful of Coastal Employment Zones, which may attract multinational firms in labour-intensive sectors from China to India. The presence of these firms will give rise to an ecosystem in which local small and medium firms will also be induced to become highly productive thereby multiplying the number of well-paid jobs.

1.21. India has, of course, already achieved considerable success in some key services and skilled-labour-intensive industries. It has had great success in the global markets in information technology (IT), information technology-enabled services (TTES) and pharmaceuticals. Its financial sector, including capital markets, has also acquired a modern character and has been exhibiting healthy growth during the past one and a half decades. Therefore, unlike past rapid transformers such as South Korea, Taiwan, Singapore and China, India has the advantage of walking on two legs: manufactures and services'. The Action Agenda offers specific proposals for jumpstarting some of the key manufacturing and services sectors, including apparel, electronics, gems and jewellery, financial services, tourism and cultural industries and real estate.

Part III: Regional Development

1.22. Chapters 7-9 in Part III focus on urban, rural and regional development, respectively. Urbanisation is an integral part of modernisation. Often, urban centres such as Mumbai and Shanghai are home to the organised sector activities. But even when uses activities locate in rural areas, they quickly turn die latter urban. Shenzhen in China offers the most striking example of such a transformation. From a group of fishing villages with a population of 300,000 in 1980, today, Shenzhen is among the most urbanised spots on the face of earth. Accordingly, the Action Agenda spells out how we can facilitate urbanisation in the country. Key challenges faced by the urban sector include affordable housing, infrastructure development, public transport, promotion of Swachh Bharat, reform of urban land markets and waste management.

1.23. A large part of India's population resides in rural areas. The challenges in the rural areas include creating jobs such mat some agricultural workers could shift to non-farm sectors, skill development, accessing education and health facilities, infrastructure, local governance, drinking water and sanitation and financial inclusion. The Action Agenda outlines possible avenues to achieve progress in these areas.

1.24. The final chapter in Part III turns to a discussion of regional strategies to achieve balanced growth across the country, such that a minimum level of prosperity comes to all. The areas covered include the North Eastern region, coastal areas, islands, North Himalayan states and desert and drought prone areas. Developing infrastructure in these areas to bridge the divide created by geographical uniqueness is an important element of government actions.

Part IV: Growth Enablers

1.25. Part IV discusses how to enhance the contribution of a number of growth enablers. These include infrastructure, digital connectivity, Public Private Partnerships (PPPs), energy, science and technology and creation of an effective innovation ecosystem, Chapters 10-15 discuss each of' these subjects in detail. Infrastructure development is one of the most crucial elements of economic transformation. The development of transport and connectivity infrastructure, including the roadways, railways, shipping & ports, in-land waterways and civil aviation, is discussed in Chapter 10. The challenges faced in this sector include physical capacity constraints, severe modal imbalances and a lack of holistic planning, maintenance and safety.

1.26. Digital connectivity has become an important driver of economic growth. In order to leverage efficiencies promised by the adoption of digital technologies, we need to develop a physical digital infrastructure network that is accessible to all. We must also create a host of software drive services including government services that can be provided digitally. The Action Agenda discusses the Digital India campaign and the actions related to enhancing digital connectivity.

1.27. Private sector involvement in infrastructure projects across different sectors helps in bridging the gap between the available public resources and the required investment. In addition, it helps in bringing private sector expertise into play. However, the institutional framework governing Public Private Partnerships (PPP) needs to be strengthened so mat bottlenecks to implementation are avoided. Chapter 12 deals with these hurdles and suggests ways to overcome men.

1.28. The energy sector is one of the key drivers of economic growth and development. Access to reliable sources of energy is a crucial issue. Chapter 13 discusses this subject including actions necessary for increasing energy Consumption and increasing energy efficiency and production. It pays particular attention to how we may improve the efficiency of distribution of coal, electricity, oil & gas, and harness renewable energy.

1.29. Another important element in India's development strategy is spurring science and technology including creating an enabling environment for innovation and entrepreneurship. With economic growth, India's contribution to science and technology' has gained some momentum but it still lags behind the other major economies in the world. A culture of innovation is also essential for India to find ways to tackle its development challenges such as access to education, improving agricultural productivity and waste water management. The Action Agenda for science and technology is presented in Chapter 14, while that for creating an effective innovation ecosystem is discussed in Chapter 15.

Part V: Government

1.30. Part V considers issues related to the government such as governance, taxation, competition and regulation. Chapter 16 discusses rebalancing the government's role in favour of public services and away from manufacturing. It also recommends reforms in the civil service, and electoral process. It suggests actions to eliminate corruption and black money, which have emerged as important policy priorities. Finally, the chapter offers suggestions for strengthening federalism and bringing states to the forefront of reform agenda.

1.31. Chapter 17 includes reforms to taxation policy and its administration with the view of reducing the scope for tax evasion and generation of black money, expansion of the tax base, and creation of a predictable and stable tax policy.

1.32. The government influences market outcomes through a regulatory environment that consists of laws, policies and rules. As elsewhere, India's regulatory environment has features that do not facilitate competition and may harm the public interest. Public procurement policies also need improvement. Chapter 18 discusses reforms that will encourage competition, improve the public procurement system and enhance the capacity of sectoral regulators.

1.33. Chapter 19 looks at the Justice System and includes a reform agenda to strengthen the rule of law in India. It covers three broad areas in which the Justice System needs reform - statutory and administrative laws, the judicial system and police. The suggestions on statutory and administrative law reform focus on modernising and weeding out old and dysfunctional elements in legislation, unifying and harmonising laws, reducing government intervention in areas where it is not required, undertaking statutory reforms in criminal justice and procedural laws, and reforming land/property related laws. The suggestions for reforming the judicial system revolve around streamlining human resource availability and performance, increasing and strengthening avenues for dispute resolution and extensive use of ICT to improve efficiency. For police reform, the important areas are state level legislative and executive reforms to help police forces serve more effectively within the modern-day democratic state.

Part VI: Social Sectors

1.34. Part VI of the Action Agenda turns to education, skill development, health and issues facing specific groups such as Scheduled Castes, Scheduled Tribes, women, children, differently abled and senior citizens. Education, skill development and health contribute to the creation of a productive workforce. Addressing the needs of all members of society is critical for inclusive growth of the country.

1.35. Given that a large and growing segment of India's population is under 25, education and skill development are critical to fully harvesting India's demographic dividend. Chapter 20 discusses the actions for improving the country's education system. The goals of improving learning outcomes in schools, raising the quality of education and research in higher education and promoting skill development are priorities for the sector. At the school level, while we have successfully brought all children into the fold of elementary education, quality education remains a distant dream. Actions to improve education quality can no longer be delayed. The chapter provides various steps to improve outcomes in the areas of school as well as higher education.

1.36. In the next fifteen years, we must entirely transform the delivery of health services and engineer a quantum jump in health outcomes. With this in view, Chapter 21 discusses measures necessary to lay down the foundation of a transformational change in the next three years. It focuses on public and preventive health, assurance of health care, reforming fiscal transfers from the Centre to states for better health outcomes, accelerating human resource development and improving access to medicines.

1.37. The guiding principle of the Prime Minister's development philosophy has been "Sabka Saath, Sabka Vikas" which implies that development should include every citizen. In this spirit, Chapter 22 discusses actions for building a more inclusive society. The chapter outlines actions aimed at the removal of obstacles faced by specific groups on the basis of gender, caste, age and physical impairment.

Part VII: Sustainability

1.38. The last part of the Action Agenda, Part VII, turns to environmental sustainability. We must address the high levels of air pollution in the cities, black carbon pollution indoors from the use of biomass fuels in cooking, massive volumes of solid waste in urban areas and deforestation. On the one hand, we must strengthen and streamline regulatory structures governing sustainability of the environment while on the other we must remove hurdles that adversely impact growth without protecting the environment. Chapter 23 outlines the action items contributing to these objectives.

1.39. Finally, water demand for irrigation, drinking and industrial use has been increasing with growth in incomes and population. But the sources of" water supply remain scarce. We must address issues such as water scarcity, uneven distribution of water resources across people, sectors and regions, deteriorating water quality and excessive dependence on groundwater. These issues are taken up in the last chapter of the Action Agenda, Chapter 24.

1.40. Only by working together towards common national goals can the Centre and stales meet India's development challenges. "Maximum Governance and Minimum Government", and "Competitive and Cooperative Federalism" are critical to achieving the full potential and creating a modern India, which brings prosperity to all of its 125 Crore citizens.

"These figures represent the Revise Estimate for Budget 2016-17"

"Asian Development Bank estimates using NSSO and ASI data".

"Panagariya, Arvind, "A Passage to Prosperity," Wall Street Journal. 14 July 2005.

Annexure 7
Prime Minister's Office: Mid-Term Appraisal of the 12th Five Year Plan

Prime Minister's Office
South Block
New Delhi-110 011

Sub.: Mid-Term Appraisal of the 12th Five Year Plan.

Reference is invited to NITI Aayog's (i) U.O. No. N-11016/19(l)/2015-CSS dated 14/12/2015; (ii) DO Letter No. VCH/I/1158/2016 dated 22/02/2016: and (iii) DO letter No. VCH/I/1206/2016 dated 18/03/2016 from Vice-Chairman, NITI Aayog on the above subject

2. In this regard, the undersigned is directed to invite attention to the following:

(i) In the Budget Speech delivered on 29.02.2016, Finance Minister: (A) has observed: *'Successive committees have questioned the merit in having Plan and Non-Plan classification of Government expenditure. A broad understanding over the years has been that Plan expenditures are good and Non-Plan expenditures are bad. This results in skewed allocations in the Budget. This need to be corrected and give greater focus to Revenue and Capital classification of Government expenditure';*

(B) has accordingly announced the Government's intention to (a) do away with the Plan and Non-Plan classification of expenditure from the fiscal 2017-18; (b) give greater focus to Revenue and Capital classification of Government expenditure; and (c) Finance Ministry would closely work with the State Finance Department to align Central and State Budgets in this matter.

(ii) Any planning cycle should factor in the periodicity of Finance Commission recommendation and political mandate (5 years of Government). It may be seen that while 12th Plan is for the period 2012-13 to 2016-17, the recommendations of 13th Finance Commission end in 2014-15 and the recommendation for 14th Finance Commission gets implemented from 2015-16 till 2019-20. Thus, there is no certainty of availability of financial resources for deciding the Central allocation for the Ministries as well to the States, Similarly, the political mandate presently is not coterminous with the plan period. Accordingly, a comprehensive new approach combining long term vision with medium term national agenda and short term action plans is required to be adopted

3. In the light of the foregoing, the undersigned is directed to convey that the Prime Minister has approved the following:

(A) Regarding the 12th Five Year Plan

(i) As the Budget for 2016-17 has been presented, NITI may update the draft appraisal document of the 12th Five Year Plan by incorporating to the extent possible: (a) consolidated physical/ financial targets for the period ending March, 2017 and (b) by considering physical performance up to 2015-16 and financial performance up to BE 2016-17.

(ii) A brief summary on learnings from the appraisal may be prepared.

(iii) The above may be completed by early June, 2016.

(iv) The draft Appraisal document of the 12th Five Year Plan incorporating items (i) and (ii) above may be brought before the Governing Council of NITI and Inter-State Council for consideration.

(B) Regarding the Future

(iv) Five years plans will be discontinued after the end of 12th Five Year Plan period. (v) A longer vision of 15 years may be formulated keeping in view the social goals set and/ or proposed and Sustainable Development Goals. (vi) To convert the longer vision into implementable policy and action, a 7 year strategy from 2017-18 may be formulated as part of a "National Development Agenda" with a mid-term review after three years. (vii) The three year timeframe from 2017-18 to 2019-20 will be aligned to predictability of financial resources during the 14th Finance Commission award period. This will also help translating into action the goals of the Government to be achieved by 2019. (viii) The above National Development Agenda should go beyond the traditional area of 'Plan' and cover the aspects of Internal Security, Defence, etc. as well and may be prepared by NITI.

(Brajendra Navnit)
Director
Tel: 2301 2613

CEO, NITI Aayog
PMO ID No. 360/31/C/38/2014-ES-II Dated:09/05/2016

Annexure 8

Sustainable Development Goals 2016-2030: 17 Goals and 169 related targets for Achievement during 2016-2030

NITI Aayog's Role

NITI Aayog has been entrusted with the role to co-ordinate 'Transforming our world: the 2030 Agenda for Sustainable Development' (called as SDGs). Moving ahead from the Millennium Development Goals (MDGs), SDGs have been evolved through a long inclusive process for achievement during 2016-2030. The SDGs cover 17 goals and 169 related targets resolved in the UN Summit meet 25-27 September 2015, in which India was represented at the level of Hon'ble Prime Minister. These SDGs will stimulate, align and accomplish action over the 15-years period in areas of critical importance for the humanity and the planet.

The task at hand for NITI Aayog is not merely to periodically collect data on SDGs but to act proactively fructify the goals and targets not only quantitatively but also maintaining high standards of quality. Ministry of Statistics and Programme Implementation (MoSPI) has already undertaken a parallel exercise of interaction with the ministries to evolve indicators reflecting the SDG goals and targets.

To achieve these tasks, the draft mapping of the goals and targets as an initial step on proposed Nodal and other Ministries has been carried out in consultation with MoSPI. Further, as an illustration, the Centrally Sponsored Schemes (CSSs) including the 'core of the core', 'core' and 'optional' Schemes being implemented by the States have been mapped alongwith some of the recent initiatives undertaken by the Central Government. In addition, Ministries are implementing Central Sector Schemes and States are also implementing various State Schemes aligned with one or more SDGs. This mapping can be accessed from the NITI Aayog site niti.gov.in.

NITI Aayog in collaboration with RIS is also holding a Consultation on SDGs, during 9th and 10th February 2016 with stakeholders including States, Ministries, academia, International organisations, NGOs etc. at New Delhi.

Goal 1: End poverty in all its forms everywhere

- Globally, the number of people living in extreme poverty has declined by more than half from 1.9 billion in 1990. However, 836 million people still live in extreme poverty. About one in five persons in developing regions lives on less than $1.25 per day.
- Southern Asia and sub-Saharan Africa are home to the overwhelming majority of people living in extreme poverty.
- High poverty rates are often found in small, fragile and conflict-affected countries.
- One in four children under age five in the world has inadequate height for his or her age.
- The all India Poverty Head Count Ratio (PHCR) has been brought down from 47% in 1990 to 21% in 2011-2012, nearly halved.

Source: URL: http://niti.gov.in/content/goal-1-end-poverty-all-its-forms-everywhere

Goal 2: End hunger, achieve food security and improved nutrition and promote sustainable agriculture

Globally, the proportion of undernourished people in the developing regions has fallen by almost half since 1990, from 23.3% in 1990-1992 to 12.9% in 2014-2016. However, one in nine people in the world today (795 million) are still undernourished.

The vast majority of the world's hungry people live in developing countries, where 12.9% of the population is undernourished.

Asia is the continent with the hungriest people - two-thirds of the total. The percentage in southern Asia has fallen in recent years, but in western Asia it has increased slightly.

Sub-Saharan Africa is the region with the highest prevalence (percentage of population) of hunger. About one person in four there is undernourished.

Poor nutrition causes nearly half (45%) of deaths in children under five—3.1 million children each year.

One in four of the world's children suffer stunted growth. In developing countries the proportion rises to one in three.

66 million primary school-age children in developing countries attend classes hungry, with 23 million in Africa alone. Agriculture is the single largest employer in the world, providing livelihoods for 40% of today's global population. It is the largest source of income and jobs for poor rural households.

500 million small farms worldwide, most still rain fed, provide up to 80% of food consumed in a large part of the developing world. Investing

in smallholder farmers is an important way to increase food security and nutrition for the poorest, as well as food production for local and global markets.

In 1990, 53% of all Indian children were malnourished. In 2015, malnourishment declined to 40%.

Goal 3: Ensure healthy lives and promote well-being for all at all ages

Child Health

- 17,000 fewer children die each day than in 1990, but more than six million children still die before their fifth birthday each year.
- Since 2000, measles vaccines have averted nearly 15.6 million deaths.
- Despite global progress, an increasing proportion of child deaths are in sub-Saharan Africa and Southern Asia. Four out of every five deaths of children under age five occur in these regions.
- India's Under Five Mortality (U5MR) declined from 125 per 1,000 live births in 1990 to 49 per 1,000 live births in 2013.

Maternal Health

- Globally, maternal mortality has fallen by almost 50% since 1990.
- In Eastern Asia, Northern Africa and Southern Asia, maternal mortality has declined by around two-thirds. But, the maternal mortality ratio - the proportion of mothers that do not survive childbirth compared to those who do - in developing regions is still 14 times higher than in the developed regions.
- Only half of women in developing regions receive the recommended amount of health care.
- From a Maternal Mortality Rate (MMR) of 437 per 100,000 live births in 1990-91, India came down to 167 in 2009. Delivery in institutional facilities has risen from 26% in 1992-93 to 72% in 2009.

HIV/AIDS

- By 2014, there were 13.6 million people accessing antiretroviral therapy, an increase from just 800,000 in 2003.
- New HIV infections in 2013 were estimated at 2.1 million, which was 38% lower than in 2001.
- At the end of 2013, there were an estimated 35 million people living with HIV.

- At the end of 2013, 240,000 children were newly infected with HIV.
- India has made significant strides in reducing the prevalence of HIV and AIDS across different types of high-risk categories. Adult prevalence has come down from 0.45 percent in 2002 to 0.27 in 2011.
- Enrolment in primary education in developing countries has reached 91%, but 57 million children remain out of school.
- More than half of children who have not enrolled in school live in sub-Saharan Africa.
- An estimated 50% of out-of-school children of primary school age live in conflict-affected areas. Children in the poorest households are 4 times as likely to be out of school as children in the richest households.
- The world has achieved equality in primary education between girls and boys, but few countries have achieved that target at all levels of education.
- Among youth aged 15 to 24, the literacy rate has improved globally from 83 per cent to 91 per cent between 1990 and 2015.
- India has made significant progress in universalising primary education. Enrolment and completion rates of girls in primary school have improved as are elementary completion rates. The net enrolment ratio in primary education (for both sexes) is 88% (2013-14). At the national level, male and female youth literacy rate is 94% and 92%.

Goal 5: Achieve gender equality and empower all women and girls

- In Southern Asia, only 74 girls were enrolled in primary school for every 100 boys in 1990. By 2012, the enrolment ratios were the same for girls and for boys.
- In sub-Saharan Africa, Oceania and Western Asia, girls still face barriers to entering both primary and secondary school.
- Women in Northern Africa hold less than one in five paid jobs in the non-agricultural sector.
- In 46 countries, women now hold more than 30% of seats in national parliament in at least one chamber. .
- India is on track to achieve gender parity at all education levels, having already achieved it at the primary level. The ratio of female literacy to male literacy for 15-24 year olds is 0.91.
- As of August 2015, in India the proportion of seats in National Parliament held by women is only 12% against the target of 50%.

Goal 6: Ensure availability and sustainable management of water and sanitation for all

- In 2015, 91% of the global population is using an improved drinking water source, compared to 76% in 1990. However, 2.5 billion people lack access to basic sanitation services, such as toilets or latrines.
- Each day, an average of 5,000 children die due to preventable water and sanitation-related diseases.
- Hydropower is the most important and widely used renewable source of energy and as of 2011, represented 16% of total electricity production worldwide.
- Approximately 70% of all available water is used for irrigation.
- Floods account for 15% of all deaths related to natural disasters.
- The overall proportion of households in India having access to improved water sources increased from 68% in 1992-93 to 90.6 per cent in 2011-12.
- In 2012, 59% households in rural areas and 8% in urban India did not have access to improved sanitation facilities. Almost 600 million people in India defecate in the open, the highest number in the world.

Goal 7: Ensure access to affordable, reliable, sustainable and modern energy for all

- 1.3 billion people - one in five globally - still lack access to modern electricity.
- 3 billion people rely on wood, coal, charcoal or animal waste for cooking and heating.
- Energy is the dominant contributor to climate change, accounting for around 60% of total global greenhouse gas emissions.
- Energy from renewable resources - wind, water, solar, biomass and geothermal energy - is inexhaustible and clean. Renewable energy currently constitutes 15% of the global energy mix.
- The total installed capacity for electricity generation in India has registered a compound annual growth rate of 7% (2013-14).
- The total installed capacity of grid interactive renewable power has been showing a growth rate of over 12% (2013-14).

Goal 8: Promote sustained, inclusive and sustainable economic growth, full and productive employment and decent work for all

- Global unemployment increased from 170 million in 2007 to nearly

202 million in 2012, of which about 75 million are young women and men.

- Nearly 2.2 billion people live below the US$2 poverty line and poverty eradication is only possible through stable and well-paid jobs.
- 470 million jobs are needed globally for new entrants to the labour market between 2018 and 2030.
- Small and medium-sized enterprises that engage in industrial processing and manufacturing are the most critical for the early stages of industrialisation and are typically the largest job creators. They make up over 90% of business worldwide and account for between 50-60% of employment.
- The unemployment rate in India is estimated to be approximately 5% at All India level (2013-14). India's labour force is set to grow by more than 8 million per year.

Goal 9: Build resilient infrastructure, promote inclusive and sustainable industrialisation and foster innovation

- About 2.6 billion people in the developing world are facing difficulties in accessing electricity full time.
- 2.5 billion people worldwide lack access, to basic sanitation and almost 800 million people lack access to water, many hundreds of millions of them in sub-Saharan Africa and South Asia.
- 1 to 1.5 million people do not have access to reliable phone service.
- For many African countries, particularly the lower-income countries, infrastructure constraints affect company productivity by around 40%.
- Manufacturing is an important employer, accounting for around 470 million jobs worldwide in 2009 - or around 16% of the world's workforce of 2.9 billion. It is estimated that there were more than half a billion jobs in manufacturing in 2013.
- Industrialisation's job multiplication effect has a positive impact on society. Every one job in manufacturing creates 2.2 jobs in other sectors.
- In developing countries, barely 30% of agricultural production undergoes industrial processing. In high-income countries, 98% is processed. This suggests that there are great opportunities for developing countries in agribusiness.
- India's growth rate averaged at 7.25% in the last 5 years.
- India's CO_2 emissions per capita are 1.67 (metric tons), one of the lowest in the world, the global average being around 4-5 (metric tons). In 2010, per capita annual electricity, consumption was 626 kwH compared to the global average of 2977 kwH.

Goal 10: Reduce inequality within and among countries

- On average - and taking into account population size - income inequality increased by 11% in developing countries between 1990 and 2010.
- A significant majority of households in developing countries - more than 75% - are living today in societies where income is more unequally distributed than it was in the 1990s.
- Children in the poorest 20% of the population are still up to three times more likely to die before their fifth birthday than children in the richest quintiles.
- Social protection has been significantly extended globally, yet persons with disabilities are up to five times more likely than average to incur catastrophic health expenditures.
- Despite overall declines in maternal mortality in the majority of developing countries, women in rural areas are still up to three times more likely to die while giving birth than women living in urban centres.
- The Gini Coefficient of income inequality for India has risen from 33.4% in 2004 to 33.6% in 2011.

Goal 11: Make cities and human settlements inclusive, safe, resilient and sustainable

- Half of humanity - 3.5 billion people - lives in cities today. By 2030, almost 60% of the world's population will live in urban areas.
- 828 million people live in slums today and the number keeps rising.
- The world's cities occupy just 2% of the Earth's land, but account for 60-80% of energy consumption and 75% of carbon emissions. Rapid urbanisation is exerting pressure on fresh water supplies, sewage, the living environment, and public health. But the high density of cities can bring efficiency gains and technological innovation while reducing resource and energy consumption.
- Cities have the potential to either dissipate the distribution of energy or optimise their efficiency by reducing energy consumption and adopting green energy systems. For instance, Rizhao, China has turned itself into a solar-powered city; in its central districts, 99% of households already use solar water heaters.
- 68% of India's total population lives in rural areas (2013-14).
- By 2030, India is expected to be home to 6 mega-cities with populations above 10 million. Currently 17% of India's urban population lives in slums.

Goal 12: Ensure sustainable consumption and production patterns

- 1.3 billion tonnes of food are wasted every year.
- If people worldwide switched to energy-efficient lightbulbs, the world would save US$120 billion annually.
- Should the global population reach 9.6 billion by 2050, the equivalent of almost three planets could be required to provide the natural resources needed to sustain current lifestyles.
- More than 1 billion people still do not have access to fresh water.
- India is the fourth largest GHG emitter, responsible for 5.3% of global emissions. India has committed to reduce the emissions intensity of its GDP by 20 to 25% by 2020.

Goal 13: Take urgent action to combat climate change and its impacts

- The greenhouse gas emissions from human activities are driving climate change and continue to rise. They are now at their highest levels in history. Global emissions of carbon dioxide have increased by almost 50% since 1990.
- The atmospheric concentrations of carbon dioxide, methane, and nitrous oxide have increased to levels unprecedented in at least the last 800,000 years. Carbon dioxide concentrations have increased by 40% since pre-industrial times; primarily from fossil fuel emissions and secondarily from net land use change emissions. The ocean has absorbed about 30% of the emitted anthropogenic carbon dioxide, causing ocean acidification.
- Each of the last three decades has been successively warmer at the Earth's surface than any preceding decade since 1850. In the Northern Hemisphere, 1983-2012 was likely the warmest 30-year period of the last 1,400 years.
- From 1880 to 2012, average global temperature increased by 0.85°C. Without action, the world's average surface temperature is projected to rise over the 21st century and is likely to surpass 3 degrees Celsius this century—with some areas of the world, including in the tropics and subtropics, expected to warm even more. The poorest and most vulnerable people are being affected the most.
- The rate of sea level rise since the mid-19th century has been larger than the mean rate during the previous two millennia. Over the period 1901 to 2010, global mean sea level rose by 0.19 [0.17 to 0.21] meters.
- From 1901 to 2010, the global average sea level rose by 19 cm as oceans expanded due to warming and melted ice. The Arctic's sea

ice extent has shrunk in every successive decade since 1979, with 1.07 million km^2 of ice loss every decade.

- It is still possible, using an array of technological measures and changes in behaviour, to limit the increase in global mean temperature to two degrees Celsius above pre-industrial levels.
- There are multiple mitigation pathways to achieve the substantial emissions reductions over the next few decades necessary to limit, with a greater than 66% chance, the warming to 2°C—the goal set by governments. However, delaying additional mitigation to 2030 will substantially increase the technological, economic, social and institutional challenges associated with limiting the warming over the 21 century to below 2°C relative to pre-industrial levels.
- India has committed to reduce the emissions intensity of its GDP by 20 to 25% by 2020.

Goal 14: Conserve and sustainably use the oceans, seas and marine resources for sustainable development

- Oceans cover three-quarters of the Earth's surface, contain 97% of the Earth's water, and represent 99% of the living space on the planet by volume.
- Globally, the market value of marine and coastal resources and industries is estimated at $3 trillion per year or about 5% of global GDP.
- Globally, the levels of capture fisheries are near the ocean's productive capacity, with catches on the order of 80 million tons.
- Oceans contain nearly 200,00 identified species, but actual numbers may lie in the millions.
- Oceans absorb about 30% of carbon dioxide produced by humans, buffering the impacts of global warming.
- Oceans serve as the world's largest source of protein, with more than 3 billion people depending on the oceans as their primary source.
- Marine fisheries directly or indirectly employ over 200 million people.
- Subsidies for fishing are contributing to the rapid depletion of many fish species and are preventing efforts to save and restore global fisheries and related jobs, causing ocean fisheries to generate US$ 50 billion less per year.
- As much as 40% of world oceans are heavily affected by human activities, including pollution, depleted fisheries, and loss of coastal habitats.
- There are some 120 species of marine mammal to be found in the world, and a fourth of these may be found in India and adjacent

countries. More than 1 million people in 3651 villages of India situated along the coast are employed in marine capture fisheries.

Goal 15: Protect, restore and promote sustainable use of terrestrial ecosystems, sustainably manage forests, combat desertification, halt and reverse land degradation and halt biodiversity loss

- Thirteen million hectares of forests are being lost every year.
- Around 1.6 billion people depend on forests for their livelihood. This includes some 70 million indigenous people. Forests are home to more than 80% of all terrestrial species of animals, plants and insects.
- 2.6 billion people depend directly on agriculture, but 52% of the land used for agriculture is moderately or severely affected by soil degradation.
- Due to drought and desertification each year, 12 million hectares are lost (23 hectares per minute), where 20 million tons of grain could have been grown.
- Of the 8,300 animal breeds known, 8% are extinct and 22% are at risk of extinction.
- As many as 80% of people living in rural areas in developing countries rely on traditional plant-based medicines for basic healthcare.
- Forest cover in India has increased to 21.23% - an increase of 5871 sq. km, and protected areas cover to about 4.8% of the country's total land area.
- India is among the early movers on the Nagoya protocol and is committed to the Aichi targets on conserving biodiversity.
- India has 8% of the world's biodiversity with many species that are not found anywhere else in the world.

Goal 16: Promote peaceful and inclusive societies for sustainable development, provide access to justice for all and build effective, accountable and inclusive institutions at all levels

- The number of refugees of concern to the United Nations High Commissioner for Refugees (UNHCR) stood at 13 million in mid-2014, up from a year earlier.
- Corruption, bribery, theft and tax evasion cost some US $1.26 trillion for developing countries per year.
- The rate of children leaving primary school in conflict-affected countries reached 50% in 2011, which amounts to 28.5 million children.

- In India, more than 20% of all pupils and one-third of all Scheduled Tribe students drop out before finishing primary education.

Goal 17: Strengthen the means of implementation and revitalize the global partnership for sustainable development

- Official development assistance (ODA) stood at approximately $135 billion in 2014,
- In 2014, 79% of imports from developing countries entered developed countries duty-free.
- The debt burden on developing countries remains stable at about 3% of export revenue.
- The number of internet users in Africa almost doubled in the past four years.
- As of 2015, 95% of the world's population is covered by a mobile-cellular signal. 30% of the world's youth are digital natives, active online for at least five years.
- Internet penetration has grown from just over 6% of the world's population in 2000 to 43% in 2015.
- But more than four billion people do not use the internet, and 90% of them are from the developing world.
- India has the second highest number of Internet users in the world, however, Internet penetration in the country is under 20%.

Annexure 9

Government of India Reduces Number of Centrally Sponsored Schemes to 28

The government has reduced the number of centrally sponsored schemes (CSS) to 28 umbrella schemes from 66, Parliament was informed today.

"Based on the recommendation of the sub-group of Chief Ministers on rationalisation of centrally sponsored schemes, the government of India has rationalised centrally sponsored schemes (CSS) effective from the financial year 2016-17.

"The schemes of CSS have been reduced from 66 to 28 umbrella schemes," Minister of State (Independent Charge) for Planning Rao Inderjit Singh said in a written reply to the Rajya Sabha.

The minister further said, "6 schemes have been categorised as Core of the Core, 20 schemes as Core Schemes and remaining two as Optional Schemes".

Expenditure Profile 2018-19 Centrally Sponsored Schemes Statement 4a

Ministry/Department	Actuals. 2016-17			Actuals. 2017-18			Actuals. 2018-19			Actuals. 2019-20		
	Revenue	Capital	Total	Revenue	Capital	Total	Revenue	Capital	Total	Revenue	Capital	Total
(A) Core of the Core Schemes	**69080.88**	**468.01**	**69548.89**	**71268.30**	**488.22**	**71756.52**	**77593.41**	**483.05**	**78076.46**	**77283.33**	**407.42**	**77690.75**
1. National Social Assistance Program	8854.07	...	8854.07	9500.00	...	9500. 00	8744.57	...	8744 57	9975.00	...	9975.00
2. Mahatma Gandhi National Rural Employment Guarantee Program	48214.95	...	48214.95	48000.00	...	48000.00	55000.00	...	55000 00	55000.00	...	55000.00
3. Umbrella Scheme for Development of Schedule Castes	4635.27	228.01	4863.28	4895.69	218.22	5113.91	4900.86	213.05	5113 91	4875.18	307.40	5182.58
4. Umbrella Programme for Development of Scheduled Tribes	3318.87	...	3318.87	3490.13	...	3490.13	3512.35	...	3512 35	3806.02	...	3806.02
5. Umbrella Programme for Development of Minorities	2650.43	140.00	2790.43	3902.49	170.00	4072.49	3905.38	170.00	4075 38	1439.98	0.02	1440.00
6. Umbrella Programme for Development of Other Vulnerable Groups	1407.29	100.00	1507.29	1479.99	100.00	1579.S9	1530.25	100.00	1630 25	2187.15	100.00	2287.15
(B) Core Schemes	**172146.57**	**52.35**	**172198.92**	**206329.31**	**347.40**	**206676.71**	**207363.88**	**141.10**	**207504.98**	**227450.64**	**375.73**	**227826.37**
7. Green Revolution	10092.53	12.53	10105.06	13687.00	54.00	13741.00	11138.84	45.82	11184 66	13795.22	113.70	13908.92
8. White Revolution	1309.16	...	1309.16	1633.97	...	1633.97	1632.97	...	163297	2219.89	...	2219.89
9. Blue Revolution	387.81	...	387.81	400.73	...	400.73	301.73	...	30173	642.61	...	642.61
10. Pradhan Mantri Krishi Sinchai Yojna	5133.43	0.56	5133.99	7375.92	1.55	7377.47	7390.77	1.37	7392 14	9427.42	1.63	9429.05
11. Pradhan Mantri Gram Sadak Yojna	17922.87	...	17922.87	19000.00	...	19000.00	16900.00	...	16900 00	19000.00	...	19000.00
12. Pradhan Mantri Awas Yojna (PMAY)	20951.69	...	20951.69	29042.81	...	2904281	29042.51	...	29042 51	27505.00	...	27505.00
13. National Rural Drinking Water Mission	5980.02	...	5980.02	6050.00	...	6050.00	7050.00	...	7050 00	7000.00	...	7000.00
14. Swachh Bharat Mission	12619.34	...	12619.34	16248.27	...	16248.27	19248.27	...	19248 27	17843.10	...	17843.10
15. National Health Mission	22869.73	...	22869.73	27116.20	15.00	27131.20	31277.06	15.00	31292 06	30631.04	3.00	30634.04
16. National Education Mission	27616.36	...	27616.36	29555.67	...	29555.67	29555.67	...	29555 67	32612.51	...	32612.51
17. National Programme of Mid Day Meal in Schools	9475.43	...	9475.43	10000.00	...	10000.00	10000.00	...	10000 00	10500.00	...	10500.00

(Contd.)

18. Umbrella ICDS	15863.32	30.00	15893.32	20716.54	38.65	20755.19	19924.10	38.65	19962 75	23088.27	0.01	23088.28
19. Mission for Protection and Empowerment for Women	793.24	...	793.24	1089.02	...	1089.02	987.50	...	987 50	1365.58	...	1365.58
20. National Livelihood Mission - Ajeevika	3486.40	...	3486.40	4849.00	...	4849.00	4699.00	...	4699 00	6060.00	...	6060.00
21. Jobs and Skill Development	1807.59	9.26	1816.85	3875.96	213.20	4089.16	2865.12	40.26	2905 38	4863.74	207.39	5071.13
22. Environment, Forestry and Midlife	794.86	...	794.86	962.01	...	962.01	975.05	...	975 05	1019.00	...	1019.00
23. Urban Rejuvenation Mission: AMRUT and Smart Cities; Mission	9276.70	...	9276.70	9000.00	...	9000.00	8998.61	...	8998 61	12169.00	...	12169.00
24. Modernisation of Police Forces	2229.85	...	2229.85	2022.00	...	2022.00	2576.95	...	2576.95	3157.29	...	3157.29
25. Infrastructure Facilities for Judiciary	541.81	...	541.81	629.21	...	629.21	629.21	...	629.21	630.00	...	630.00
26. Border Area Development Programme	1015.00	...	1015.00	1100.00	...	1100.00	1100.00	...	1100.00	770.97	...	770.97
27. Shyama Prasad Mukherjee Rurban Mission	599.44	...	599.44	1000.00	...	1000.00	600.00	...	600.00	1200.00	...	1200.00
28. Rashtriya Swasthya Bima Yojna	1379.99	...	1379.99	975.00	25.00	1000.00	470.52	...	470.52	1950.00	50.00	2000.00
(C) Others	452.26	...	452.26	...	...	...	...	...	...	...	...	...
29. Others	452.26	...	452.26	...	...	...	...	...	...	...	...	...
Grand Total	**240775.19**	**520.36**	**241295.55**	**277597.61**	**835.62**	**278433.23**	**284957.29**	**624.15**	**285581.44**	**304733.97**	**783.15**	**305517.12**

Annexure 10

Guidelines for District Plans in the Eleventh Five Year Plan

No, M-13011/1/2006-SP-Coord.
Planning Commission
(State Plans Division)

Subject: Guidelines for District Plans in the Eleventh Five Year Plan

I. Introduction

The need for integrated local area plans, based on specific endowments and needs of each area, was stressed from the beginning of planned development in 1950s. However, despite several reports and studies, there were only sporadic efforts and isolated cases of such planning. Development was mostly done through sectoral schemes and programmes of a uniform nature, resulting in limited outcomes and wastage of resources. The constitution 73rd and 74th Amendments mandated local planning at the village panchayat, intermediate panchayats and district panchayat levels as well as in urban local governments and their consolidation into a District Plan in each district. Though more than fourteen years have gone by since the constitutional mandate was brought into effect, there has been little progress except in very few states.

It has been decided that the 'district plan process' should be an integral part of the process of preparation of state's Eleventh Five Year Plan (2007-2012) and the annual plan 2007-2008. With this in view, the Ministry of Panchayati Raj constituted an Expert Group in 2005, in consultation with the Planning Commission.

The Report of the Expert Group on planning at the grassroots level was presented to government in March 2006. It has been accepted by the Ministry of Panchayati Raj and the Planning Commission and was circulated the States in April-May 2006. Attention is drawn to Chapter 3 of the Report.

This circular deals with the further steps to be taken as part of the preparation of the states' draft Eleventh Five Year Plan/Annual Plan 2007-2008, proposals.

II. District Planning

District Planning is the process of preparing an integrated plan for the local government sector in a district taking into account the resources (natural, human and financial) available and covering the sectoral activities and schemes assigned to the district level and below and those implemented through local governments in a state.

The document that embodies this statement of resources and their allocation for various purposes is known as the District Plan. It would essentially have three aspects namely:

1. Plan to be prepared by the Rural Local Bodies for the activities assigned to them and the national/state schemes implemented by them with their own resources and those earmarked for these purposes;
2. Plan to be prepared by the Urban Local Bodies for the activities assigned to them and the national/state schemes implemented by them with their own resources and those earmarked for these purposes;
3. Physical integration of the plans of Rural and Urban Local Bodies with the elements of the State Plan that are physically implemented within the geographical confines of the district.

All the three aspects would be considered and consolidated by the District Planning Committee (DPC) into a District Plan.

Quite obviously, the District Plan cannot be prepared in isolation, and must take into account and respond to the expected activities of the non-government sector of the local economy.

Important among these would be:

1. Plan emerging from activities of people's groups like SHGs, Co-operatives etc.
2. Plan emerging from the financial institutions like the local branch (es) of Commercial Banks (both in the public and the private sector), NABARD, Co-operative Banks and the like.
3. Plans of International Non-Governmental Organisations (INGOs)/ NGOS and Bilateral Agencies operating in the District.
4. Plans of other private agents that would either have an impact on the activities of the government or would need the government to respond to those developments insofar as its own areas of functioning/service delivery are concerned.

III. Steps to be taken at State Level

The State Governments (State Planning Commission/Board/Department) may take urgent steps for the following, **if not already done:**

1. Complete the assignment of **Activities** to be undertaken by different levels of local governments;
2. Form District Planning Committees (DPC) as envisaged in the constitution, that is, with 80% members being elected from the elected members of the Panchayat and urban local governments in each district and the remaining 20% being nominated by the state governments; preferably with experts.
3. Issue guidelines to the DPC and local governments generally on the lines indicated in Section IV below;
4. Decide on the formula for distribution of local government component of the state plan and indicate the broad order of resources that would be available to different levels (and therefore to each local government) over the five years/one year (2007-08) from the state plan - this would be sector-wise as well as untied;
5, Indicate the resources that would broadly be available to each local government from central sources through centrally sponsored schemes, special allocations, including those by Finance Commissions, etc;
6. Prepare the draft District Plans and after vetting, present a summary of District Plans, in the format indicated in Section IV, along with State Plan proposals for the Eleventh Five Year Plan/ Annual Plan 2007-08.

IV. Preparation of District Plan

In the preparation of the draft district plan, the various steps detailed in Chapter 3 of the Report of the Expert Group on Planning at the Grassroots Level may be generally followed. (Provided as Annexure-I). The present state of development and the resource endowment including capability vary widely across states. It is not necessary to wait for perfection or latest technology to get started with the process. Separate steps may be taken to improve internal capabilities.

The following steps are suggested:

1. The available data may be put together for each local government. The state government agencies, the departments and the district statistical organisations (central and state) should assist them in this. Some of the essential items of data are listed in the suggested form at Annexure-II.
2. Based on the data, a vision document for 10 to 15 years is to be prepared by the district and for each local government based on a participatory assessment. The DPC may hold formal interactions with local governments and other key stakeholders on this and

then finalize it. The document should clearly identify the key reasons for backwardness/ development shortcomings and address issues impeding development. It will cover:

- Agriculture and allied sectors (as relevant)
- Availability and development of water sources
- Industries - especially traditional, small industries including food processing
- Infrastructure including power
- Drinking water and sanitation
- Literacy, school education
- Health and medical facilities
- Poverty reduction and basic needs
- Gender and children
- Social Justice - SC/ST, Persons with disability etc.

3. To assist the DPC in preparing the vision document (and subsequently to vet the draft plan proposals), a Technical Support Group may be constituted in each district. It may consist of departmental officers (where available) mandated and nominated for the purpose in addition to their duties or retired persons locally available or a local academic institution or established NGO with a proven record - Similarly, technical support as appropriate, may be organised for the urban areas, intermediate panchayats and village panchayats.
4. If undertaken in a campaign mode, the preparation of vision documents can be completed in two months' time.
5. Further, if District is to be the economic unit for planning exercise, the scope of **vision** document could be expanded to include areas of comparative advantage of each district (availability of technical institutions, BPO, tourism, agro-industry, etc.), which would be the basis for attracting private investment.
6. Based on the vision document/s and following the same participatory process, the needs may be prioritised and goals set for a five-year period for a draft five year plan in the manner indicated below:
   a) The draft plan preparation should start at the Gram Sabha level. The Gram Panchayat may finalize its Plan based on priorities emerging from the Gram Sabha and give suggestions for the Intermediate Panchayat. Projects and activities which can be implemented at the Gram Panchayat Level should be included as "Gram Panchayat Plan". Those projects and activities which can be implemented only in more than one Gram Panchayat, will be forwarded to the Intermediate Panchayats to be considered for inclusion into the "Intermediate Panchayat Plan".

The Gram Panchayat Plans should also provide an estimate of the community contribution that can be mobilised for the purpose of implementing the development plan.

b) Based on these suggestions received from Gram Panchayats and its own priorities the Intermediate Panchayat should finalize its Plan. Projects and activities which can be implemented at the Intermediate Panchayat Level should be included as "Intermediate Panchayat Plan". Those projects and activities which need to be implemented in more than one intermediate Panchayat will be forwarded to the District Panchayat to be considered for inclusion into the "District Panchayat Plan",

c) Based on the Gram Panchayat Plans, the Intermediate Panchayat Plans and District Panchayat Plans, the District Planning Committee shall finalize the District Plan for the District.

d) A similar exercise may be undertaken in Urban Local Governments. Each local government may be asked to give separate suggestions for inclusion in the Departmental components of the District Plan.

7. The time limit for different steps, in para 6 above, needs to be indicated. Similarly, timeframe for integrating District Plans with State Plans also needs to be indicated in view of limited time available for the beginning of Eleventh Five Year Plan.
8. The draft plan proposals of each local government should be in accordance with the approved Activity assignment and the centrally-sponsored flag-ship and related programmes (as and where applicable).
9. The draft plan proposals will cover the sectors mentioned in (2) above and will indicate the expected outcomes in terms of production, employment, infrastructure and human development.
10. While preparing the draft plan in accordance with (6), (7), (8) and (9) above, the concerned local government will take into account the district component of the departmental plans as also the Centrally Sponsored Schemes and the Externally Aided Projects that have been assigned to it for implementation. In addition, the physical integration of the District Plan with the elements of the State Plan that are being implemented in the geographical area of the district would need to be given close attention. The resources and outlays in respect of these items of State Plan located in the district (but not implemented through the local bodies) would not, however, be included in the Plan Resources and outlays of the Local Bodies.
11. The local government component of the District Plan would emerge out of the resource envelope containing the following sources of funds:-

a. Own resources available for development
b. Transfers by State Finance Commission for development purposes
c. Twelfth Finance Commission grants passed on by the State Government.
d. Untied grants for local planning.
e. Grants in respect of Centrally Sponsored Schemes that have been assigned to the local bodies for the purposes of implementation.
f. Grants for State Plan schemes assigned for implementation through Local Governments.
g. Grants for Externally supported schemes assigned for implementation through Local Governments.
h. Estimated contribution by the communities themselves.

12. The DPC will consolidate the two streams the Panchayat plans and the urban area plans, integrate them with the departmental plans for the district and prepare the draft five year plan and the Annual Plan.
13. The State Planning Commission/Board/Department may issue the above as guidelines and suggest the broad structure of the district plan document and the forms to be annexed to the document.

V. Presentation as part of State's Eleventh Plan Proposals

1. A summary of the District Plans will have to be presented as part of the State's Eleventh Five Year and Annual (2007-08) Plan proposals.
2. For this purpose, a Note on the present status of empowerment of local governments and the procedures adopted in getting local draft plans prepared by all levels of local governments will be attached to the plan proposals.
3. Summary statements will be presented in the attached Annexure-III formats in addition to the forms usually adopted for State Plan Proposals. (The forms refer to Annual Plan could be the same for five year plan).
4. The sum total of the outlay on District Plans in a state may be around 40 percent of the gross state plan outlay*.

(Avtar Singh Sahota)
Director (SP-Coord.)
25.08.2006

---

* 'Gross' Plan outlay includes central share of centrally sponsored schemes. It is, thus, State Plan Outlay Central Share of CSSs.

Planning Secretaries of States/UTs

Copy to:

1. Principal Advisers/Advisers/ Heads of Divisions in Planning Commission.
2. PS to Deputy Chairman / Members / Member-Secretary

Copy also to:

1. Secretary, Ministry of Panchayati Raj, Krishi Bhavan, New Delhi.

Annexure 11

Second Round Table of State Minister of Panchayati Raj, Mysore, 28th-29th August, 2004

Ministers in charge of Panchayati Raj, and their representatives, bearing in mind the spirit of cooperative federalism which must inform the effective implementation of Panchayati Raj as set out in Para-IX of the Constitution of India and related provisions, including in particular, Article 243ZD (District Planning Committees), agreed to recommend to their respective Governments, for joint acceptance by the Centre and the States, the following points of action:

I. Planning

1. There shall be constituted in every State, at the district level, a District Planning Committee (DPC) by the end of the current financial year wherever such DPCs do not already exist.
2. All DPCs should be constituted according to the procedure laid down in the Constitution in Article 243ZD(2).
3. All States must make provision, by law, for the functions relating to District Planning Committees.
4, District planning must take into account:
   (i) resource endowment of the area:
   (ii) felt needs of the people ; and
   (iii) relative absorptive capacity.
5. As provided for in the Constitution, each tier of the Panchayati Raj system - Village, Intermediate and District - must prepare the perspective Five Year Plan and Annual Plans for their respective jurisdiction. The same exercise should be undertaken in the Municipalities of each district. The DPC should "consolidate" the plans prepared by the Panchayats and Municipalities, as provided for in the Constitution, rather than prepare the District Plan of its own accord or of its own volition.
6. To fine-tune the plans prepared at different levels, as also to undertake the consolidation of plans in the DPC in a technically acceptable sense. State Governments, in accordance with the provisions of Article 243ZD (3) (b), may specify institutions, organisations and individuals, who may assist the Panchayats. Municipalities and DPCs in preparing plans of a technically acceptable nature.

7. To facilitate such planning, the State Government in accordance with the provisions of Article 243ZD, may indicate to each level of the Panchayats and Municipalities, "the extent and type of available resources, whether financial or otherwise".
8. To the extent possible, resources should be made available to the Panchayats and the Municipalities on an untied, general purpose basis. Where grants are tied to schemes, guidelines should be broad and simple so that they are readily understood by elected representatives at the Panchayat and Municipality level.
9. Recognising the financial constraints under which most State Governments at present operate, the primary responsibility for providing untied grants and simplified schemes rests with the Union Government and the Planning Commission. The Central Government may, therefore, consider establishing a mechanism at the Centre which will pool together all the Central Government and Finance Commission's resources with a view to channellising as large proportion of these as possible to the PRIs through the District Rural Development Agencies (DRDAs) which might be renamed as the District Panchayat Development Agencies (DPPAs) since they will be receiving all the resources of the Central Government rather than just those of the Ministry of Rural Development alone. In any case, wherever State Governments have abolished DRDAs, and merged them with Zilla Panchayats, this channel may be used. The proposed DPDA may be so merged with the District Panchayat that its resources, both financial and in terms of technical manpower, are made available to all tiers of the Panchayati Raj system in accordance with the activity maps prepared by the State Governments for each tier of the Panchayati Raj system.
10. Thus, even as in the case of the devolution of functions, functionaries and finances, planning at each level of the PRIs may be undertaken in accordance with activity mapping.
11. The States, depending upon their resource availability, might appropriately strengthen the sound finances of the PRIs so that planning at the District and Sub-District level is based on an indication of the resources available and those that would be made available, for the activities devolved on them.
12. In the budgets of State Governments, besides the traditional division between the State sector and the District sector, consideration may be given to incorporating a Panchayat sector in each departmental budget. At the Centre, the Planning Commission, in consultation with the Central Ministries concerned, might work out similar appropriate arrangements.

13. In allotting financial resources to PRIs, the distinction between administrative grants and development grants may be maintained.
14. State Governments may consider incorporating in their State laws provision for the formation of Standing Committees within each Panchayat body to undertake the responsibilities relating to planning and implementation for the subjects allotted to them. These Committees could have an earmarked budget, based on the Panchayats allocating funds to the Standing Committees, depending on their respective responsibilities.
15. In the preparation of District Plans, priority should be given, first, to plans for the provision of basic minimum needs; second, to the provision of services: third, to facilitating Rural Business Hubs; and, fourth, to general economic development.
16. The Planning Commission is requested to ensure that the 11- Plan begins with and is founded on District Plans prepared in accordance with the provisions of Part-IX and IXA of the Constitution.

II. Implementation

1. As institutions of local government, Panchayati Raj Institutions are required to not only plan but also to implement such programmes of economic development and social justice as may be "entrusted" to them, including those in relation to the matters listed in the Eleventh Schedule. As such, points relating to implementation parallel those relating to planning. What applies to planning applies *pari passu* to implementation.
2. Article 243G of the Constitution provides for the implementation of schemes to be "entrusted" to PRIs. This means entrusted schemes should be implemented by PRIs and not by line departments.
3. For the effective implementation of entrusted schemes, chairpersons must act as "chairperson - in-council". There must be full activation of subject-related Standing Committees of the Panchayat so that all elected members of the Panchayat participate in managing all aspects of implementation, from conception to approval; from the calling of tenders to the fmalisation of vendors; and from conducting supervision of on-going works to certifying the issue of utilisation certificates. Of course, the Gram Sabha needs to be involved in every stage of the process.
4. Effective implementation also requires that the Gram Sabha plays an active role in auditing both the physical and financial performance of the Gram Panchayat's plans, programmes and

projects, as also "entrusted" schemes. Three major functions of the Gram Sabha should be incorporated in the legislation of States:

(i) Selection of beneficiaries;

(ii) Approval of plans, programmes and projects prepared by the Panchayats;

(iii) Authorize the issue of Utilisation Certificates after having verified the progress of a work. It is crucial that the Gram Sabha's social audit functions be written into the law.

5. The adoption of a Citizens' Charter, the Right to Information by law and community- based movements such as *Jan Sunwais* have been found to be greatly effective aids in the exercise of the effective devolution of powers and responsibilities to the PRIs. It is, therefore, recommended that a time-bound plan be put in place, along with a built — in system of checks and balances, for ensuring transparency and community participation in the working of the Panchayats.

III. Parallel Bodies

1. The devolution of functions, functionaries and finances, based on activity mapping, is required by the Constitution (Article 243 G) to be devolved to **only** the Panchayats and **not** to any parallel body.
2. If, for reasons of institutional constraints, parallel bodies have been set up or are to be set up, these must be brought into an organic, symbiotic relationship with the PRIs at the appropriate level so that PRIs are fully involved with the work of the parallel bodies.
3. To the extent possible, parallel bodies should be established only where indispensable, and invariably in consultation with, and with the collaboration of the PRIs at the appropriate level.
4. By law, parallel bodies should be required to report periodically to the Gram Sabha(s) so that the community as a whole is kept informed of the activities of parallel bodies.
5. The Central and State Governments may evolve modalities and mechanisms for granting permission to parallel bodies, including those established by foreign and multilateral donor agencies, so that parallel bodies do not undermine the Constitutional authority of PRIs as "institutions of self-government" but work together to their mutual benefit and the common benefit of the community.

Annexure 12

State Finance Commission

Article 243I of the Indian Constitution prescribes that the Governor of a State shall, as soon as may be within one year from the commencement of the Constitution (Seventy-third Amendment) Act, 1992, and thereafter at the expiration of every fifth year, constitute a Finance Commission to review the financial position of the Panchayats and to make recommendations to the Governor as to

A. The principles which should govern

1. The distribution between the State and the Panchayats of the net proceeds of the taxes, duties, tolls and fees leviable by the State, which may be divided between them under this Part and the allocation between the Panchayats at all levels of their respective shares of such proceeds;
2. The determination of the taxes, duties, tolls and fees which may be State Finance Commissions assigned as, or appropriated by, the Panchayats;
3. The grants-in-aid to the Panchayats from the Consolidated Fund of International Experience the State;

B. The measures needed to improve the financial position of the Panchayats;

C. Any other matter referred to the Finance Commission by the Governor in the interests of sound finance of the Panchayats.

Article 243Y of the Constitution further provides that the Finance Commission constituted under Article 243 I shall make similar recommendation vis-a-vis municipalities.

The Governor is required to cause every recommendation made by the State Finance Commission together with an explanatory memorandum as to the action taken thereon to be laid before the Legislature of the State.

Links to the websites of the State Finance Commissions wherever established are provided below:

States			
Andhra Pradesh	Arunachal Pradesh	Assam	Bihar
Chhattisgarh	Goa	Gujarat	Haryana
Himachal Pradesh	Jammu & Kashmir	Jharkhand	Karnataka
Kerala	Madhya Pradesh	Maharashtra	Manipur
Meghalaya	Mizoram	Nagaland	Mizoram
Punjab	Rajasthan	Sikkim	Tamil Nadu
Tripura	Uttaranchal	Uttar Pradesh	West Bengal
Union Territories			
Andaman & Nicobar Island	Chandigarh	Daman & Diu	Delhi
Dadra and Nagar Haveli	Lakshadeep	Puducherry	

Annexure 13

Government of India. Appointment Committee of the Cabinet O.M. dated 20th Number, 2017: Appointment of Prabhari Officers for 115 Backward Districts

No. 7/3/2017-EO(SM-I)
Government of India
Secretariat of the

New Delhi, the 20th November, 2017

OFFICE MEMORANDUM

Subject: Appointment of Prabhari Officers for 115 Backward districts

The undersigned is directed to refer to the above mentioned subject and to say that senior officers at the level of Additional Joint Secretaries are hereby appointed as Prabhari Officers on behalf of Government of India for coordinating the efforts of the Centre and States in achieving rapid transformation of identified 115 backward districts by addressing their specific developmental needs. The above initiative is in consonance with the Prime Minister's vision of a "New India' by 2022. The 115 backward districts have been identified based on select indicators of backwardness and prevalence of Left Wing Extremism, etc. (The list of officers nominated as Prabhari Officers indicating their districts also is enclosed at **Annexure I**). The Prabhari Officers will work in a collaborative manner with the State and District teams to achieve effective convergence between various Central and State Government programmes. Steps are also being taken to establish a comprehensive database and an efficient feedback mechanism.

2. CEO, NITI Aayog has already written to the Chief Secretaries of various *States/UTs* in this regard (Copy of his letter is at **Annexure II**). For launching this initiative, a Workshop is being organised on 24th November at **CSOI Auditorium, New Delhi** which will be chaired by the Cabinet Secretary. All Prabhari Officers are required to attend the Workshop in which the details of this initiative will be discussed.

3. The officers may kindly be directed to reach the venue of the Workshop by **10.30 AM** on **24th November, 2017.** For any clarifications, they may contact Shri Rakesh Ranjan, DDG (Evaluation) & Sr. Consultant, NITI Aayog (Tel: 011-23042095 / 23096558 / +91-9999038591; email: ranjanrakesh100@gmail.com).

P.K. Tripathi
Establishment Officer & Additional Secretary
Tel: 23092370

To,

1. All the Secretaries to the Government of India (as per list attached)
2. All the Chief Secretaries of the States (as per list attached)
3. All the administrators of UTs (as per list attached)

Copy for information to:

1. CEO, NITI Aayog
2. Cabinet Secretariat (Shri G. Aramane, Additional Secretary), Rashtrapati Bhawan, New Delhi.

Annexure 14

Transforming 115 Backward Districts Across the Country, First Meeting of Prabhari Officers on 24th November 2017

Press Information Bureau
Government of India
NITI Aayog

23-November-2017 19:15 IST

In keeping with the Prime Minister Narendra Modi's vision of a New India by 2022, Government has embarked upon a major policy initiative for the rapid transformation of 115 backward districts across the country. Senior Government officials in the rank of the rank of Additional Secretary and Joint Secretary have been designated as Prabhari Officers or the in-charge to coordinate the efforts of the Centre and the states in addressing the specific developmental needs of the districts.

The First meeting of the Prabhari Officers entrusted with the responsibility to co-ordinate the efforts of the Centre and the States towards rapid transformation of 115 backward districts across the country will be held tomorrow on Friday, the 24th November. Cabinet Secretary, PKSinha will chair the meeting with the CEO of the NITI Aayog, Amitabh Kant. Secretaries of key Ministries would also attend this session, Home-Secretary will also brief the Prabhari Officers, Among the 115 backward districts, 35 are affected by Left Wing Violence, Shortly after this event, meeting of representatives of the State Governments and Prabhari officers is being organised to ensure that transformation of backward district in India is carried out by a dedicated team of Central and State governments.

Background

The Prime Minister Shri Narendra Modi has given a Vision for a new and vibrant India by 2022, the year when India celebrates its 75th year of Independence. Inclusive development and improving the liveability of all are integral part of this vision. One of the initiatives in this regard is to make a dramatic improvement in overall socio-economic development of backward districts. The strategy envisaged is to adopt a focussed approach, ensure convergence of efforts of the Central, State and local Government and establish a real time monitoring mechanism to focus on outcomes that matter to common people in these districts beside giving rise to a virtuous cycle of economic development.

A total of 115 districts have been identified for this purpose on the basis of objective criteria. Such criteria include education, health, nutrition basic infrastructure like rural road connectivity, rural household electrification, access to potable water and individual toilets, etc. These districts include 35 districts which are affected by violence by Left Wing Extremists. Besides, while selecting these districts, it has been ensured that Ministries of Government of India, implementing social sector Scheme would select at least one most backward districts in every State for extending the reach of the programme in different part of the country. Improvement in one district is likely to spur similar growth in neighbouring districts through demonstration effect.

Under this initiative, for all these 115 districts, senior level Government officers (Additional Secretary/Joint Secretary) have been nominated as Prabhari officers. It has been envisaged that using their experience, these officers would form a team with representatives of the State Governments and would also act as a bridge between Centre and the State. States have been accordingly requested to nominate senior level functionary for each district. States are the main drivers of this program.

Annexure 15

Press Information Bureau Govt. of India 02 January, 2012 Backward Regions Grant Fund

Press Information Bureau
Government of India
Special Service and Features

02-January-2012 16:23 1ST

The Backward Regions Grant Fund Programme (BRGF), launched by the Prime Minister at Barpeta in Assam on 19th February 2007, signifies a new approach to addressing persistent regional imbalances in development. The programme subsumed the Rashtriya Sama Vikas Yojana (RSVY), a scheme earlier being administered by the Planning Commission. The BRGF Programme covers 250 districts in 27 States, of which 232 districts fall under the purview of Parts IX and IX-A of the Constitution dealing with the Panchayats and the Municipalities, respectively. The remaining 18 districts are covered by other local government structures, such as Autonomous District and Regional Councils under the Sixth Schedule of the Constitution and state specific arrangements as in the case of Nagaland and the hi!! areas of Manipur.

Objectives

The Backward Regions Grant Fund is designed to redress regional imbalances in development by way of providing financial resources for supplementing and converging existing developmental inflows into the identified backward districts, so as to:

- Bridge critical gaps in local infrastructure and other development requirements that are not being adequately met through existing inflows,
- Strengthen, to this end, Panchayat and Municipality level governance with more appropriate capacity building, to facilitate participatory planning, decision making, implementation and monitoring, to reflect local felt needs,
- Provide professional support to local bodies for planning, implementation and monitoring their plans,
- Improve the performance and delivery of critical functions assigned to Panchayats, and counter possible efficiency and equity losses on account of inadequate local capacity.

The BRGF programme represents a major shift in approach from top-down plans to participative plans prepared from the grassroots level upwards. The guidelines of the Programme entrust the central role in planning and implementation of the programme to Panchayats in rural areas, municipalities in urban areas and District Planning Committees at the district level constituted in accordance with Article 243 ZD of the Constitution to consolidate the plans of the Panchayats and Municipalities into the draft district plan. Special provisions have been made in the guidelines for those districts in J&K, Assam, Manipur, Meghalaya, Mizoram, Nagaland and Tripura which do not have Panchayats, where village level bodies and institutions mandated under other frameworks such as the Sixth Schedule are to plan and implement the programme. The conviction that drives this new locally driven approach is that grassroots level democratic institutions know best the dimensions of poverty in their areas and are, therefore, best placed to undertake individually small, but overall, significant local interventions to sustainably tackle local poverty alleviation.

There are three features of BRGF that make it truly unique among central initiatives to combat backwardness. First, the approach of putting the Panchayats and the Municipalities at the centre stage of planning and implementation. Second, no Central funding stream is as 'untied' as the BRGF - the funds can be applied to any preference of the Panchayat/ Municipality, so long as it fills a development gap and the identification of the work is decided with people's participation. Third, no other programme spends as much funds, nearly 11 percent of the total allocation, for capacity building and staff provisioning,

District planning, which commences from the level of each local body and is finally concluded at the district level through the consolidation of these local Panchayat and Municipality based plans by the District Planning Committee into the draft district plan, is expected to better strategise both local and more wide ranging interventions into a composite strategy document.

Creation of capacity for effective planning at district and lower level is a key-pre-requisite to participative planning. Hence the BRGF contains a specific component for the capacity building of Panchayati Raj Institutions of Rs. 250 crore per year. A framework that looks upon capacity building in a very comprehensive fashion, encompassing training, handholding and providing ongoing support to Panchayat elected representatives has been developed for States to follow, while undertaking capacity building.

The planning process under BRGF is based on the guidelines for district planning issued by the Planning Commission in August, 2006 and January, 2009. The process of integrated development commences with each district undertaking a diagnostic study of its backwardness and a baseline survey by enlisting professional planning support, to be followed by a well-conceived participatory district development perspective plan to address this backwardness during the period of the Eleventh Five Year Plan. Such plans would integrate multiple programmes that are in operation in the district concerned and, therefore, address backwardness through a combination of resources that flow to the district.

BRGF Development Grants

District Plans received from the various States indicate that the untied fund allocated to the districts are generally being used for filling infrastructural gaps in drinking water, connectivity, health, education, social sectors, electrification, etc. The basket of works taken up includes construction of school buildings /class rooms, health sub-centres, drinking water facility, sanitation facilities, anganwadi buildings, Panchayat buildings, irrigation tanks/channels, street lights, link roads, culverts, soil and water conservation measures, etc.

BRGF Capacity Building Grants

The BRGF has adopted the National Capability Building Framework (the NCBF) which envisages strengthening of institutional arrangements, including the infrastructure as well as software support for capacity building of elected representatives, the functionaries and other stakeholders of PRIs and thereby improving the vigour of grassroots level democracy.

During the current financial year, district plans have been received from 223 districts. Except for Jharkhand, where DPCs have been constituted only in the month of December, 2011, all States having BRGF districts have forwarded plans duly approved by the DPC or a body at the district level mandated under the BRGF guidelines to approve the plans. BRGF funds are being used for critical gap filling in respect of infrastructure and human development indices. As on date, Rs. 1830.13 crores for both Development Grant and Capacity Building have been released for 2011-12, another Rs. 110.25 crores has been sanctioned while an amount of Rs. 428.5 crores is under process.

In 2009, the World Bank conducted an independent evaluation of the BRGF programme in 16 districts in 8 States. The key findings of the evaluation were that though the funds allocated under BRGF are small, meaningful investments are made by the communities in projects that are chosen in a decentralised participatory manner. The evaluation report pointed out that the BRGF funds are the single most important source of discretionary funds available to the Panchayats. The study also suggested that outlays should be enhanced in order to be more effective.

With inputs from Ministry of Panchayati Raj
SS-01/SF-01/02-01-2012
RTS/HSN

Annexure 16

Application for Obtaining Information u/s 6(1) of the Right to Information Act, 2005

Speed Post/E-mail

K.D. Saksena I.A.S. (Retd.)
Former Secretary to Govt, of India,
Ministry of Textiles, Chairman, NIFT
- Member, B.I.F.R./Company Law Board
- Adviser, Union Planning Commission
- Economic Planner, Bhutan (UNDP)

44, Din Apartments, Sector-4,
Plot No. 7, Dwarka Phase-I
New Delhi-110078
Tel.: 011-45531344, M: 9868209537

Date: 18.04.2018/01.05.2018

To
Shri V. Sridhar, Under Secretary & Head of Office
Central Public Information Officer
Cabinet Secretariat NACWC
Rashtrapati Bhavan, New Delhi

Subject: Application for obtaining information u/s 6(1) of the Right to Information Act, 2005.

Dear Sir,

An Indian Postal Order of Rs. 10/- payable to the Accounts Officer Cabinet Secretariat, Govt, of India is enclosed.

2. The following information / certified copies of documents may kindly be made available to me on payment of the prescribed fee. I may be informed about the total amount payable and the mode of payment to enable me to pay the required amount.

(i) A copy of the 'Cabinet Note' in which the Cabinet Resolution No. 11/2/2015-Cab dated 1st January, 2015 was proposed to come into effect from the 1st day of January 2015 superseding the Cabinet Resolution No. l-(P(C)/50 dated the 15th March, 1951 setting up the Planning Commission.

(ii) Were any consultations made on the proposed subsequent Cabinet Resolution or approval obtained from:

(a) National Development Council;
(b) Inter-State Council with whom the recommendations of the Sarkaria Commission relating to the Planning Commission are pending consideration;
(c) Both Houses of the Parliament;
(d) Chief Ministers of all States and UTs;
(e) Concerned Ministries of the Govt, of India, such as Ministry of Planning, Ministry of Finance, Home Ministry, Ministry of Panchayati Raj/ Rural Development, Ministry of SCs / STs and Ministry of Social Welfare.
(f) Consultation Committee of the Ministry of Planning.

If so, copies of the letters issued to them and replies received, indicating the action taken thereon may kindly be made available.

(iii) Copies of the 'Cabinet Notes' as originally drafted and as subsequently amended in the light of the responses/communications received from the institutions/persons mentioned in sub-para ii).

(iv) Copy of the minutes of the Cabinet Meeting in which the Cabinet approved the supersession of the earlier Cabinet Resolution dated the 15th March, 1950 setting up the Planning Commission by a Cabinet Resolution dated the 1st January, 2015 setting up NITI AYOG in its place with the constitution and functions as per this subsequent Resolution.

Yours faithfully,

End.: Postal Order of Rs. 10/- (K. D. Saksena)

Annexure 17

Proposal for Replacing Planning Commission and Passing a New Resolution Setting up the National Development and Reforms Commission

Secret

File No. 43011/64/2014-Admn.I
Government of India
Planning Commission

Copy No.
New Delhi-11000 1
13 August, 2014

Note for Cabinet

Subject: Proposal for replacing the Planning Commission and. passing a new Resolution setting up the National Development and Reforms Commission

Introduction

1. This is a proposal to replace the Planning Commission in its current form and pass a Cabinet Resolution setting up a National Development and Reforms Commission (NDRC).

Background

2. The Planning Commission was constituted in pursuance of an announcement made by the Finance Minister in the Budget Speech on 28.2.1950 by means of a Government of India Resolution. The Resolution, inter alia, mandated the Commission to strive to further the principles of policy enshrined in Article 39 of the Constitution (Part-IV Directive Principles of State Policy). Further, it was envisaged that the Planning Commission will make recommendations to the Cabinet. In framing its recommendations, the Commission would act in close understanding and consultations with the Ministries of the Central Government and the Government of the States. A copy of the Resolution is at **Annexure-I.** The

list of past Chairpersons, the Deputy Chairpersons and Members of the Planning Commission is at **Annexure-II.**

3. The roles and responsibilities of the Planning Commission as laid down in the GOI Resolution of 1950 were subsequently included in the Allocation of Business Rules, 1961. Entry 49 relates to Planning Commission and lists over a dozen functions and charge of attached offices such as UIDAI and National Rainfed Area Authority, Economic Advisory Council and Institute of Applied Manpower Research. Entry 26 relates to the Ministry of Planning, viz., *'the responsibility to Parliament with regard to subjects of National Planning'*. It may be mentioned however, that **'Economic and Social Planning' is part of List-III (Concurrent List) of the Constitution** (Entry 20).

Evolution of the Functions of the Planning Commission

4. The functions of the Planning Commission were laid down in the GOI Resolution of 1950 in paragraph 4. Inter-alia, the functions included:

a. **Assess the resources** of the country and investigate possibilities of augmenting such of these resources as are found to be deficient in relation to the nation's requirements;
b. **Formulate a Plan** for the most effective and balanced utilisation of country's resources;
c. Based on priorities, **define the stages** in which the Plan should be carried out and propose the allocation of resources;
d. Determine the **conditions for the successful execution** of the Plan;
e. Determine the **nature of the machinery** needed for successful implementation of the Plan;
f. **Appraise** from time to time the progress achieved and recommend adjustments that may be necessary;
g. Make such **interim or ancillary recommendations** as appear to it to be appropriate.

5. Over the years, the Planning Commission has evolved and has taken on a number of additional functions (detailed description at **Annexure III).** Some of the major ones are:

a. Building a **long term strategic vision** of the future and decide on priorities of nation. It works out **sectoral targets and provides promotional stimulus** to the economy to grow in the desired direction.
b. Play **an integrative role in policy formulation,** e.g., in energy, transport, rural development, health, education, etc. An integrated approach can lead to better results at much lower costs.

c. Focus on **efficiency of utilisation** of allocations being made.
d. Play **a mediatory and facilitating role** between Ministries and between Centre and States.
e. Play **a** systems change role and provide consultancy within the Government for developing better systems (e.g., in PPPs).

Weaknesses in the current functioning of the Planning Commission

6. While the Planning Commission has evolved to perform far more functions than originally envisaged, a number of questions have been raised both about its structure, role and processes followed in the context of its functions as well as the changes in the national landscape. One of the primary changes that has led to this critique is that the country has moved to a freer market economy with a smaller role both for the public sector and public allocation of resources. Serious questions have been.raised about the planning function in the modern market economy in a globalized world.

7. In its 35th Report, on Demand for Grants (2011-12) the Standing Committee on Finance of the 15th Lok Sabha had observed that Planning Commission *"has to come to grips with the emerging social realities to re-invent itself to make itself more relevant and effective for aligning the planning process with economic reforms and its consequences, particularly for the poor".*

8. The former Prime Minister, Dr. Manmohan Singh, in his farewell address to the Commission in April 2014, had also raised the following issues, and urged introspection:

> *"India's development story is a work in progress. The Planning Commission has played a historic role in this story so far. But there is a lot of distance that is still to be covered.*
>
> ***The external world is changing rapidly. The structure of the economy and the role of the state in the economy are also changing.*** *With an increasingly open and liberalized, economy with a greater reliance on market mechanisms, we need to reflect on* ***what the role of the Planning Commission needs: to be in this new world.***
>
> ***Are we still using tools and approaches which were designed for a different era?***
>
> ***Have we added on new functions and layers without any restructuring of the more traditional activities in the Commission?***
>
> *What additional roles should the Planning Commission play and what capacities does it need to build to ensure that it continues to be relevant to the growth process?*

Governance issues being integral to economic growth, are these areas for the Planning Commission to delve into?"

These are pertinent questions that go deep into the role and functions of this body in the current stage of economic development.

9. The Planning Commission is a relic of the era when Central Planning for resource allocation was dominant in development economic philosophy. Most countries which adopted centralised state-controlled planning and allocation of resources have themselves moved on into newer approaches far more suited to the current times. USA, which is one of the most open economies, depends to a great extent on think tanks for policy design inputs. They are thought leaders and the government draws on them heavily for specific purposes. However, there is limited planning in a mandated sense of allocation of resources. In Japan, METI (the Ministry of Economy, Trade & Industry, formerly famously known as MITI) coordinates industrial activities and energy security by providing long range forecasts and plays a coordinating function. It works closely with the private sector to ensure that national objectives are achieved. China too has moved away from the State Planning Commission model.

10. There have been other criticisms about the functioning of the Planning Commission, particularly from the states. The relations of the Planning Commission with states at times has been acrimonious. There have been concerns that rather than the Finance Commission, the Planning Commission is becoming an arbiter of resource sharing with states. There have been many recommendations on removing the distinction between Plan and Non-Plan as well. All this has led to a shrinking fiscal space for states, loss of flexibility in designing and implementing their own developmental programmes which are often perceived to be more effective and a disconnect with outcomes as emphasis has been on spending financial allocations so that future "Plan sizes" are not cut. Annual Plan meetings have also become rituals.

Abolition of the Planning Commission and setting up a National Development and Reforms Commission (NDRC)

11. In view of the above, there is an adequate case for abolishing the Planning Commission in its current form. It has outlived its utility and the context of its constitution has changed drastically.

12. However, there is a case for having a national body which performs a set of functions which are essential for economic development. This body, which could be called the **National Development and Reforms Commission (NDRC)** could perform, inter alia, the following functions (details in **Annexure IV**):

a. **Promote co-operative federalism** and become an instrument for systematic and structured interaction between the Union Government and State Governments. The NDRC can enable or facilitate periodic structured discussions between the two, both formally and informally to understand multiple perspectives on common developmental issues and forge a consensus on strategies and implementation mechanisms. Particular attention will be paid to the needs of smaller states and remote and inaccessible states.

b. **Develop National Development Strategies,** both sectoral and cross-sectoral, with a view to achieving national developmental goals, with a focus on structural issues and policy reforms that are conditions precedent to the achievement of these goals. The emphasis would be on an integrated, holistic cross-cutting approach across all departments. In this process, Ministries of the Central Government and States would be assisted in developing their own medium-term and long-term visions, goals and strategies for themselves.

c. **Engage in perspective planning** with an analytical, longer term view over a few decades, analysing global and domestic trends and assessing their implications for current development strategies and identifying areas that need focused attention in the shorter term to respond to these trends.

d. Prepare frameworks for the design of programmes and schemes to ensure that basic programme design principles with a focus on results are adhered to. The frameworks would contain parameters for decentralisation, delegation and flexibility to states and implementing agencies so that desired outcomes are achieved. These would also include identifying performance metrics and measuring these to assist in budget allocations.

e. **Develop methodologies for decentralised planning andl decision-making,** in tune with the constitutional scheme of Central and State Governments, Urban Local Bodies and Panchayati Raj Institutions.

f. **Bring greater efficiency and impact into development programmes** through a strong monitoring and evaluation function. This would include a reduction in the number of Centrally Sponsored Schemes, bringing in flexibility into their operational guidelines, incentivising state governments to experiment and innovate with their own approaches.

g. **Develop an internal consultancy function** for the Government, both at the Centre and States. This would be built on specialised skills which are common for a wide-range of applications such as Public Private Partnerships, Project Appraisal, Monitoring of

Performance Metrics, Evaluation of Programme Impact, and other areas where it is inefficient to replicate these in each Ministry or agency. States would be an important clientele for this internal consulting resource.

h. **Provide specialised inputs to the Prime Minister** and the government on matters referred to it requiring detailed analysis and specialized inputs either from within the Government or from outside.

i. **Engage with** think-tanks **and other** academic **institutions** involve them closely in its functions, particularly in designing strategies and in monitoring and evaluation. Involvement of these bodies would be part of the programme design frameworks to be laid down by the NDRC, with an emphasis on generating hew ideas and approaches and having these mainstreamed into government policies and programmes.

j. **Create subordinate bodies for specific functions** as and when necessary in pursuit of the above goals, providing flexibility to the government system.

Structure of the National Reforms and Development Commission

13. The NDRC can have a lean structure as follows:

i. **Chairman,** being the Prime Minister.

ii. **A Deputy Chairman,** nominated by the Prime Minister and who will function in a **full-time** capacity.

iii. **Upto 8 Members,** nominated by the Prime Minister and who will function either in a **full-time or part-time** capacity. The number and areas of specialisation would be based on functional needs.

Location of NDRC, its Organisation, and Processes

14. The NDRC will be located in the current premises of the Planning Commission. It would take over the staff, assets and Budget of the Planning Commission and modify these to suit its mandate.

15. The Planning Commission has grown into an unwieldy body performing additional functions without reviewing and restructuring its organisation. It has added new functions and new layers in its organisation without any structural changes. The NDRC will be given the leverage to reform its structure to suit its mandate. It will be given the flexibility to change staff designations, roles, functions and their appointment procedures. The emphasis throughout will be on functionality, flexibility, domain knowledge and a focus on meeting its mandate. The NDRC will also develop a **strong monitoring and evaluation function** with necessary

skill-sets in its staff so that **these functions which are currently spread over many bodies can take place in one body.** This may require abolition or merger of other bodies into the NDRC.

16. The NDRC will develop new approaches for interaction with states in the spirit of co-operative federalism. It will move away from existing structures which are outmoded to more equitable and focused processes including at regional levels so as to enable effective dialogue on common development concerns of the Centre and States.

Justification

17. The need for replaving Planning Commission and the justification for a National Development and Reforms Commission have been explained in paras 6-10 above.

Inter-Ministerial Consultation

18. The matter will be discussed directly in the Cabinet as it concerns the repealing of an earlier Cabinet resolution and setting up a new body through a fresh resolution.

Approval Sought

The approval of the Cabinet is sought to:

a. Repeal the Cabinet Resolution of 15th March, 1950 setting up the Planning Commission (at **Annexure-I)**
b. Pass the Resolution at Annexure IV establishing the National Development and Reforms Commission (NDRC) with the functions laid down in the Resolution and described at paragraph 12 of the Note.

19. The Statement of Implementation Schedule is at **Appendix-I.**

20. A statement on Equity, Innovation and Public Accountability is attached at **Appendix-II.**

21. The above Note has been seen and approved by the Prime Minister.

Sindhushree Khullar
Secretary, Planning Commission
Tele No. 23096574

Annexure 18

Note for Cabinet. Implementation of Cabinet Decision dated 13th August, 2014 Setting Up the National Institution for Transforming India (NITI Aayog)

Secret
File No. 43011/64/2014 Admn.1
Government of India
Planning Commission

Copy No........
New Delhi-110001

29th December, 2014

Subject: Implementation of Cabinet decision dated 13th August, 2014 setting up the National Institution for Transforming India [NITI Aayog]

1. Introduction

1.1 Gandhiji had once said "If you realize that all things change, there is nothing you will try to hold on to". Reflecting this spirit and the changed dynamics of a new India, the institutions of governance and policy have to adapt to the changes in the state of the economy and the role of the State. The proposal to set up a new Institution called National Institution for Transforming India [NITI Aayog] is in accordance with this spirit of change.

2. Background

2.1 The Cabinet at its meeting on 13th August, 2014 approved the, repeal of the Cabinet Resolution dated 15th March, 1950 setting up the Planning Commission. The Cabinet also authorized the Prime Minister to make such changes as considered necessary in the light of the deliberations in the draft Resolution annexed to the Note for Cabinet. The decision of the Cabinet dated 13th August, 2014 is at **Annex-1** (page 13 of the note).

2.2 Consequent to this decision, the Prime Minister in his address to the nation on 15th August, 2014 outlined the raison d'etre for setting up the new Institution. Relevant extracts of the Prime Minister's address to the nation on 15th August, 2014 is at Annex 2 (page 14 of the note)

2.3 Immediately after the address by the Prime Minister on Independence Day, 2014 the process of undertaking extensive consultation for designing the new Institution was initiated. As people of India are the most important stakeholders, suggestions were invited on *MyGov.in* web portal. The portal contained an Open Forum on which suggestions for composition, structure and roles of the new Institution were invited. In addition, the portal had a Creative Corner for receiving suggestions regarding name, logo and taglines of the new Institution.

2.4 There was an overwhelming public response on this portal. More than 2900 suggestions were received on Open Forum. In addition, about 4000 + suggestions were received in Creative Corner.

2.5 On 26th August, 2014, consultations were held with experts, eminent persons and former Members of the Planning Commission, in brainstorming meetings organized at the Planning Commission. Suggestions were received in these meetings and also in papers sent by the participants underlined the need for setting up a new Institution. The suggested tasks of the new Institution included appropriate arrangement for strengthening interaction between States and Centre in economic sphere for ensuring synergy in economic development, setting up of a think tank for providing input to the Government for an informed policy making, preparation of a blue print for a long term strategy in key economic sectors like energy, transport, urban transformation, rural development including agriculture transformation, human development including education, skill development, health and nutrition, issues related to water and land, competitiveness of manufacturing, etc. It was also suggested that the new Institution should play a major role in appraisal of important Government schemes and programmes, in their monitoring, and finally, in their evaluation, to ensure that the benefits of development are reaching the people. Another specific suggested task of the new Institution was to facilitate upgradation of technology in different processes to make the economy more competitive on a sustained basis. It is also to bo stated that there was a consensus, that for making the new Institution effective, it must be chaired by the Prime Minister. A gist of suggestions received from the eminent expert is placed at Annex-3. (page 15 to 17 of the note)

2.6 Detailed papers/responses have also been received from Think Tanks, renowned individuals and sectoral experts as well as concerned citizens. On the vision for a new Institution, the suggestions included in these papers are also on similar lines to the suggestions received during the brainstorming meetings. In addition, there has been extensive analyses, comments and suggestions in the print and electronic media on the decision to replace Planning Commission which have been collated and taken on board.

2.7 To take the consultation process further, on 7th December, 2014, the Prime Minister met the Chief Ministers (CMs) to elicit their views. The resolve of the Union Government to strengthen cooperative federalism by forming suitable teams of the Central Government and the States at various levels for development was the underlying spirit of this consultation. Broad areas in which suggestions were invited included structured mechanism of interaction between the Centre and the States, changes required in the planning processes in the country, development of the New Institution as a Think Tank and suggestions on flow of Central development assistance to the State Plans. In the meeting there was a consensus that the consultation mechanism between the Centre and the States needs to be strengthened as the existing forum of the Planning Commission and the NDC did not address the specific needs of the States or a group of States. Further, they neither provided a satisfactory channel for discussion nor a platform for consideration of differences across States on development issues. It was observed that NDC meetings had become rituals and did not allow meaningful interactions. In addition, Central assistance to State Plans had become strait-jacketed with little flexibility to the specific requirements of the States. A gist of the suggestions made by the CMs in the meeting is placed at **Annex 4 of the note, (pages 18-19 of the note)**

3. Justification

3.1 The Planning Commission was set up on the 15th March, 1950 through a Cabinet Resolution. Nearly 65 years hence, the country has become an emergent economy in an increasingly globalized world, with one of the largest economies in the world, and a citizenry with a vastly different and higher level of aspirations in terms of progress and governance. The inputs received from the consultative process mentioned in para 2.3 to 2.7 clearly indicated a need for setting up a new Institution. The changing nature of the economy and various imperatives for ensuring the future transformation of the country are summarized below:

3.1.1 The Indian economy has become more open and integrated with the world, in fact, it is an increasingly important factor in the performance trajectory of the global economy. Developments in the Industrial and Service sector as well as the progress in agricultural production have provided a strong foundation to the economy. To build further on this base, the new India needs a governance paradigm where the government is an "enabler" rather than a "supporter of first and last resort".

3.1.2 Many themes contribute to the changed dynamics in the new India. But they are driven and held together by the development of technology, and specifically, the revolutionary change in the access to and sharing of information.

3.1.3 The pool of entrepreneurial, scientific and intellectual human capital is a source of power waiting to be unleashed to help us attain unprecedented heights of success. Technology and information access have shaped ambitions of the various elements that make up the country and accentuate the unity in diversity that defines the country. Various regions, states, cultures and eco-systems have spawned varied aspirations - yet often all pulling in the same direction. To realize the full power of her inherent diversity, India needs a development model that is more; consensual and co-operative, across states, regions and all the elements of the governance structure. A shared vision of national development has to be agreed upon, based on ensuring that progress is inclusive and sustainable and all are sought to be provided a life of dignity and self-respect.

3.1.4 The challenges faced by the country are also more complex. The potential of India's youthful demographic has to be realized, through education, employment and opportunity. The people have to get the right institutional and infrastructure support that, allows them to compete internationally and play their rightful part on the global stage.

3.1.5 However, despite the change the primary role of the government in achieving national objectives will continue. It will set policies that anticipate and reflect the country's requirements and then deliver them in a just manner to the citizens. In essence, the requirement is for governance and government that is vigorous and vibrant, adaptive and participative, while being responsive to the needs of a "plugged in" population that aspires to move the country into the domain of the developed world.

3.1.6 Governance, across the public and private domains, is now the concern of society as a whole. Everyone has a stake in ensuring the public good. In the past, governance may have been rather narrowly construed as public governance. In today's changed dynamic with delivery of public services often in the hands of private entities, and a higher scope for a participative citizenry through technology, governance encompasses and involves everyone.

3.1.7 Improvement of governance is, therefore, a pre-requisite for improving the quality of life of the people. Equally, it can only be achieved by a creative, synergistic and constantly evolving partnership between all stakeholders across the public and private sectors, as well as civil society.

3.1.8 In the context of governance structures, this indicates the need for setting up an institution" that serves as a "think tank" for the government, a directional and policy dynamo. Therefore, the proposed institution should provide the governments at the Central and State levels with relevant strategic and technical advice across the spectrum of key elements of policy. This would include matters of national and international import on the economic front, dissemination of best practices, from within the country, as well as from other nations, the infusion of new policy ideas and specific issue based support.

4. Proposal

4.1 On careful consideration of the changing requirement of the economy, the present context of development and the need for transparent governance, the inputs received during consultations and all other facts, it is felt that the framework for interaction between the Centre and States must be robust, active and led from the front by the Central and State leadership together. It is, therefore, proposed to set up a **Prime Minister's Council of Chief Ministers** by an executive order replacing the Resolution dated 15th March, 1950 setting up the Planning Commission and the Resolution dated 6th August, 1952 setting up the National Development Council and its subsequent reconstitution vide Resolution dated 7th October, 1967. A key differentiator from the past will be to discard a Central to State one way flow in favour of a genuine and continuing partnership with the States. **The New Institution will be called National Institution for Transforming India [NITI Aayog].**

Objectives of NITI Aayog

4.2 Swami Vivekananda said "Take up one idea. Make that one idea your life - think it, dream of it, live on that idea. Let the brain, muscles, nerves, every part of your body, be full of that idea and just leave every other idea alone. This is the way to success".

4.3 In line with this spirit, it is reiterated that the NITI Aayog will be the incubator for the ideas that will take the country to the next level of development. Through commitment to a co-operative federalism, egalitarian access to opportunity, participative and adaptive governance and by continuously increasing use of innovative technology, it will seek to piovide a critical directional and strategic shill to the processes of governance.

Functions

4.4 The National Institution for Transforming India [NITI Aayog] is being set up with the following functions:

(a) To evolve a shared vision of national development, its priorities, sectors and strategies, with the active involvement of the States. This shared vision will then provide a framework national agenda which will be given impetus by the Prime Minister and Chief Ministers together;

(b) To foster co-operative federalism recognizing that strong States make a strong nation through structured support to the States on a continuous basis;

(c) To design strategic and long term policy and programme initiatives, ensure their appraisal and implementation, monitor their progress and evaluate their effectiveness. The lessons learnt through monitoring and feedback will be used to make inventive improvements including necessary mid-course corrections and become a repository of best practices in sustainable, inclusive development;
(d) To render policy advice, create a support system for knowledge, innovation and entrepreneurship through collaboration with national and international experts, practitioners and other relevant parties;
(e) To encourage partnerships between key stakeholders and with national and international think-tanks, educational and policy research institutions;
(f) To offer a platform for resolution of inter-sectoral and inter-departmental issues in order to accelerate the implementation of the national development agenda;
(g) To maintain a state of the art Resource Centre, research on good governance and help dissemination of the same to stake-holders;
(h) To actively over-see the implementation of programrnes and initiatives, including identification of the resources required to strengthen outcomes and scope of delivery;
(i) To focus on technology up-gradation and capacity development in development programmes and initiatives; and
(j) To undertake **such other** activities as **may be necessary in** order **to further the implementation of the national development agenda, and the** objectives **above.**

Composition of NITI Aayog

4.5 The National Institution for Transforming India [NITI Aayog] will comprise **the following:**

(a) Prime Minister of India as the Chairperson.
(b) Governing Council including Chief Ministers of all States and Lt. Governors of Union Territories.
(c) Regional Councils to address specific issues related to the various regions comprising the Chief Ministers of States and Lt. Governors of Union Territories in the region, based on their needs, to focus on specific issues from time to time. The Regional Councils will be chaired by the Prime Minister.
(d) Experts, specialists and practitioners with relevant domain knowledge as Special Invitees nominated by the Prime Minister.

4.6 The full-time organizational framework will function as the Secretariat for the Governing Council and the Regional Council. It will comprise, in addition to the Prime Minister as the Chairperson,

(i) *A Vice-Chairperson:* To be appointed by the Prime Minister.
(ii) *Full-time Members:* To be appointed by the Prime Minister.
(iii) *Part-time Members:* Maximum of 2 from leading universities research organizations and other relevant institutions in an ex-officio capacity to be appointed by the Prime Minister. Part-time Members will be on a rotational basis.
(iv) *Ex-officio Members:* Maximum of four Members of the Central Council of Ministers to be nominated by the Prime Minister from time to time.
(v) *Chief Executive Chief Operating Officer:* To be appointed by the Prime Minister for a fixed tenure in the rank of Secretary to the Government of India.
(vi) Secretariat as deemed necessary.

4.7 The Headquarters of the National Institution for Transforming India [NITI Aayog] will be in New Delhi.

5. Inter-Ministerial Consultation

5.1 No Inter-ministerial Consultation is required as the Cabinet in its meeting held on 13th August, 2014 had authorized the Prime Minister to make such changes regarding the structure and function of the new institution, as considered necessary, in the light of the deliberations.

6. Approval Sought

6.1 The proposals at paras 4.1 to 4.7 are placed for information and confirmation of the Cabinet. A Resolution laying down the objectives, functions and the structure and composition of the National Institution for Transforming India [NITI Aayog] as proposed in paras 4.1 to 4.7 would be notified separately. Consequential changes required in the structure and functions of the Planning Commission would be given effect to accordingly.

7. The statement of Implementation Schedule is **at Appendix-I. (page 11 of the note)**

8. A statement on Equity, Innovation and **Public** Accountability **is** attached **at Appendix-II. (page 12 of the note)**

9. The above Note has been approved by the Prime Minister.

(Sindhushree Khullar)
Secretary, Planning Commission
Tele No. 23096574

No. 57/CM/2014
Cabinet Secretariat
Extracts From The Minutes Of The Meeting Of The Cabinet Held At 1500 Hours, On Monday, 29th December, 2014, **In** Panchavati, 7, Race Course **Road, New Delhi.**

Case No. 354/57/2014 **Other Item 5**

Implementation of Cabinet decision dated 13th August, 2014 setting up the National Institution for Transforming India [NITI Aayog].

The Cabinet considered the note dated 29.12.2014, circulated in the meeting, from the Planning Commission (Yojana Aayog) and approved the proposal contained in paragraph 6.1 thereof.

Secret

In accordance with the rules of Procedure in Regard to Proceedings of the Cabinet (Rule 10), progress of the action to implement the decision may be included in the Ministry's Monthly Summary for the information of the Members of the council of Ministers.

Action taken to implement the decision may be communicated to the Cabinet Secretariat with reference to the Implementation Schedule attached to the agenda note.

Annexure 19

Plan Coordination and Management Division: Gist of Inputs Received During Brainstorming Sessions on August, 2014

Secret

(Para 2.5 of page 3 of the note)
File No. 43011/64/2014 Admn.1
Government of India
Planning Commission

No. M-12017/08/2014-PC
Planning Commission
(Plan Coordination & Management Division)

Brainstorming Session was organized comprising a wide range of experts/ex-members/eminent persons on 26/8/2014 at Yojana Bhawan. It was held in two separate groups simultaneously comprising eight persons each to seek inputs on the role, functions and structure of the new institution. The main recommendations of the two groups are summarized below:

2. Expectations

(i) The New Institution (NI) should be relevant in the current economic context where the country is an open economy in a globalized world. It is also the largest functioning democracy. The NI should not limit itself to the financial resources of the government sector but must also focus on the private sector and private investment. **Its main focus should be the elimination of poverty and provision of basic services.**

(ii) The **NI** should be an effective interface between the Centre and the States especially as a major portion of Central assistance to States through Plan is currently flowing through Centrally Sponsored Schemes (CSS).

(iii) The NI should be capable of working towards **a** "smart functioning government of 21st century as a high powered think tank" and a knowledge hub that would sponsor and undertake policy research and strategy analysis. It must provide inputs on major policy issues in key areas like **Energy, Water, Land use, Environment, Transport, Urbanization, Trade Investment and Technology.**

(iv) The NI should have the capacity to analyze global trends in key areas including technology and investment. In this connection, it should be able to recognize challenges to the national economy, provide an early warning for looming macro economic threats and identify opportunities for global engagement in all areas of the economy.

3. Structure

(i) The NI must function under the Prime Minister and derive its mandate, authority and powers from the Prime Minister. Therefore, the Prime Minister shall be the Chairman of the NI.

(ii) As an effective interface between the Centre and the States, its role as the Secretariat of the National Development Council (NDC) must be strengthened. There was a view that the NI must take over the Secretariat of the Inter State Council which should be placed under the charge of the Prime Minister. The Inter State Council was constituted in 1990 under Article 263 of the Constitution and owes its origins to recommendation adopted in June, 1949 by the Constituent Assembly.

(iii) Coordination, monitoring, evaluation and the implementation on the ground must be strengthened.

(iv) Recommendations of the Think Tank should flow into public policy directly through Prime Minister's Office/Cabinet. Another view was that it should also be available in public domain for all to access.

(v) However, it was unanimously agreed that the structure of the proposed NI would depend on its functions.

4. Functions

(i) There was a unanimous view that the allocation of annual plan resources to the States should be transferred to the Ministry of Finance. The devolution of finances to the States must continue as a function of the Finance Commission and there should be absolutely no change in its role and mandate.

(ii) However, there were grave concerns that in case the allocation function is transferred to the Ministry of Finance, the benefit of an independent and at times an adversarial view about the prioritization of development expenditure would not be available to the Prime Minister. The Ministry of Finance, in its current form, does not lend itself to a qualitative appreciation of the imperatives of development. Moreover, in case the functions are transferred, "the Think Tank will have no teeth".

(iii) The CSS should be reduced to a minimum of 12-15 schemes in critical areas of national importance and, moreover, should be funded 100% by the Centre with effective monitoring and evaluation of outcomes.

5. Composition

(i) The NI should be a compact body comprising very few full time Members and several Part Time members. The Part Time members could serve for fixed terms of 1 to 2 years drawn from Industry, Science Academia etc. and could also be rotated amongst the Chairman/Head of the State Planning Boards of General Category States and Special Category States.

(ii) The Economic Development Board of Korea (including the Korean Development Institute), the Planning Body of Singapore (RAHS) and NDRC of China were suggested as role models.

(iii) The NI could also be modelled on the National Security Council with a mirror body like NSCS/NSAB and a National Development Advisor (NDA) serving in the Prime Minister's Office. The Economic Advisory Council must be subsumed within the NI.

(iv) Some names that were suggested are:
 (a) Development Commission
 (b) Sustainable Development Commission
 (c) National Development Advisory Board
 (d) Agency for Planning, Development and Reforms

6. Reorganisation Internal Structure

(i) The NT should be cross sectoral and cross ministerial in nature. It should continue to mediate inter-sectoral priorities amongst Central Ministries and its policies. The infrastructure Ministries like Transport and Energy, in particular, require a unified approach to resolution of key issues facing the economy.

(ii) The Quality of existing personnel and potential staffing was a concern. The ability of a government body to be able to attract international level experts was moot given the scales of government compensation packages. It was felt that if the "Think Tank" has to establish credibility, there has to be some flexibility in being able to recruit appropriate personnel.

(iii) The staffing should be such that persons from Academia, Government, Industry and experts with domain knowledge are attracted and brought on the same platform with attractive packages. However, they should be able to express their views freely and leave for their existing organizations at will.

GIST OF VIEWS OF CMS (DECEMBER 7, 2014)
CO-OPERATIVE FEDERALISM

There was a consensus among the Chief Ministers, regarding the need to integrate cooperative federalism in the New Institution. The Chief Ministers from, Haryana, Maharashtra and Rajasthan spoke about the need to create smaller groups amid States, to streamline economic development. It was suggested the States be divided into groups based on their regions or specific requirements, for instance, the categories could be expanded thus, arid region, coastal, Himalayan states, etc. All the Chief Ministers from the North Eastern States voiced their concerns regarding the special category states, and how it is imperative for the Union Government to continue providing targeted assistance to these states.

Planning Including Perspective Planning

There was no consensus regarding the five year plans. Most of the Chief Ministers welcomed the idea of making medium and long term plans. In welcoming this idea, the Chief Ministers felt that there was a need to do strategic planning, given the dynamic economic scenario. Some of the CMs suggested that planning horizon of different sectors may be different. The Chief Minister of Goa felt that there should be two separate plans respectively, for a long term strategy and a shorter plan of 1-3 years with regard to immediate needs.

A section of Chief Ministers, like CM, Himachal Pradesh and Tripura, felt that the live year plans should be continued.

Innovation and Knowledge Hub

All the Chief Ministers were in concurrence with the new Institution including an innovation and knowledge hub. Most Chief Ministers felt that this hub should be a repository of best practices that can be shared across states. The sectors/themes that need focus under this hub include PPP, external financing, technological developments and human development. It was also agreed upon that monitoring and evaluation should be an important function of the new institution.

Flow of Central Assistance to State Plans

The Chief Ministers preferred that a larger per cent than what it is at present of the Central assistance should come in the form of untied block grants. Also, most Chief Ministers felt that the CSS should be made more flexible and their number should be limited. The States wanted more autonomy in expenditure related to the subjects under State List. Some Chief Ministers also stated that distinction of Plan and Non-Plan Expenditure should be removed.

Index